Back There, Then

Linda C White!

BACK THERE,
THEN

A historical genealogical memoir by

Marietta Stevens Crichlow

with notes by Linda Crichlow White

Marietta S. Crichlow

ISBN: 978-1-938205-13-2
Library of Congress Control Number: 2014942182

Printed in the United States of America
Published by Blackwell Press, Lynchburg, Virginia

**BLACKWELL
PRESS**

Contact Blackwell Press at;
311 Rivermont Avenue
Lynchburg, Virginia 24504
434-528-4665
Email: Sales@BlackwellPress.net
www.BlackwellPress.net

We hope you enjoy this family story. If you have clues about additional family history or just want to talk about the folks mentioned herein, send an e-mail to lindacrichlow@aol.com or call 202-607-7392.

For updates see www.backtherethen.com

TABLE OF CONTENTS

ACKNOWLEDGMENTS

First, to Marietta Crichlow for having the foresight to take as many notes as she could about the family and for writing them down! Thanks to cousin Carolyn Brown for saving and sharing the Lynchburg portion of the Glover, Garland, and Brown families. Thanks to cousin Donna Crichlow for sparking the family's interest in Cyril Crichlow's connection with Marcus Garvey. Thanks to Professor Robert Hill for eagerly following up with our family then sharing information about Cyril Crichlow that is in the Marcus Garvey Archives at UCLA. Thanks to cousins Konnetta Simons Alexander (a certified genealogist), Lois Simons Benson, and Alfonzo Allen for assistance with the Crichlow-Warnick-Simons part of the story. Thanks to Vernestine Laughinghouse of Absolute Organizing Solutions and Jody Al-Saigh of Picture Perfect Organizing for their assistance with organizing all the letters, photos and other STUFF!

Thanks to Nicholas J. Kersten, librarian-historian of the Seventh Day Baptist Historical Society in Janesville, Wisconsin, who provided much information about Cyril and Lillian Crichlow and their work with the Seventh Day Baptists. Thanks to the other librarians and archivists who helped or inspired: Christopher Erman at the Library of Congress, John Muller at DC Public Library, and Dr. Ida Jones of the Howard University Moorland-Spingarn Research Center, Leslie Anderson of the Alexandria Public Library, and Midge Elliott of the Amherst County Museum and Historical Society. Thanks to the African American Historical and Genealogical Society—DC, Prince Georges County, and National chapters for the instruction and inspiration! Thanks to Gail and Kay Hansberry for helping to review the manuscript in its various stages.

Thanks to Patrick Schroeder, Appomattox Park Historian who personally showed us around the Appomattox National Park and who shared information about Wilmer McLean from the Appomattox Park Library.

Thanks to so many others who have written and shared their family stories including Appomattox resident Beatrice Pierce James and librarian Elizabeth Brumfield who wrote about her plumber step-father, inspiring me to gather more information about Martin Crichlow, the plumber.

Thanks to Nancy Blackwell Marion of Lynchburg's Blackwell Press who saw this project to completion *and* helped research the family history. Her knowledge of Lynchburg history is unsurpassed!

Special thanks to my favorite librarian and husband, Eric White, who scanned many images, made photocopies, drove me to Lynchburg, and lent support in so many ways.

And thanks to Kwame and Khalila and all the other descendants who we hope will appreciate and carry on the stories.

FOREWORD

The life of African American people during the twentieth century is written in numerous media. There are photographs, oral histories, moving footage, and newspapers. The unique voice of life amongst the masses is often swept together during the Great Migration, Depression, World Wars, and civil rights era.

Rarely, has the unique voice of an average life successfully lived been documented. In the case of Marietta Louise Stevens Crichlow, such a life continues to live on in the pages of her meticulous notes. Her daughter, Linda Crichlow White, has painstakingly linked the past with the present in a spectacular fashion. Written in the first person, Mrs. Crichlow's story follows her family from places such as Appomattox and Lynchburg, Virginia; to Duquesne, Pennsylvania; Washington, DC; Boston, and beyond. Howard University figures prominently.

Beautifully accented with photographs of ancestors, original documents, and scholarship, Mrs. White presents African American life in real time and feel. Her mother, Mrs. Crichlow, wrote: "Prior to having electricity installed, the house had gas lights. Gas lamps were fastened to the walls. And the streets had gas lights." She also wrote "None of the high school personnel talked with me about attending college. There were no school counselors in those days. Two adults lived next door to us, Vernon and his brother, Frank Worrell. Frank had attended Howard University…but dropped out for lack of funds. It was Frank who suggested that I apply for admission to Howard." She attended Howard and graduated in 1941. On the occasion of her 30th high school reunion, out of the 14 Colored students, four attended college, which was unusual since women in 1930s America were expected to marry and raise children. This reminiscence is accompanied by a Latin Club photograph where the three brown faces stand out against the 20-plus white ones.

Throughout the narrative, education, faith, and family figure prominently. The primary source materials of certificates, college degrees, photographs, and church programs bring the reader into world of the Crichlow clan while on the campus of Howard University, funeralizing a loved one, welcoming a baby, or dealing with day-to-day life. In this work we see ourselves reflected in human possibility and our potential evident in the growth of a successful American family, living as African American citizens.

By Dr. Ida E. Jones, Ph.D.
Assistant Curator
Manuscript Division
Moorland-Spingarn Research Center
Howard University

PREFACE

This document was substantially written by Marietta Stevens Crichlow in the 1990s. It was "discovered" in 2009 while planning for Marietta's 90th birthday celebration as Linda was looking through Mom's voluminous cache of photo albums and other memorabilia.

Mom had diligently typed her memories of family members and events and bound them in a looseleaf binder with Xeroxed copies of photographs, but no page numbers or index. A couple of years later, and with the help of professional organizers, I found the originals to most of the copies and scanned them for a more professional look.

The history of African Americans continues to unfold. Regrettably, we have too often been depicted as slaves, drug users, good-timers, and rabble rousers in various states of subjugation, deprivation, misery, and squalor.

Marietta Stevens, ca. 1966

Linda believes that Marietta and our extended family represent the majority of African Americans and that we fit into none of the aforementioned categories. Our ancestors have been hard-working, self-supporting people who believed that God was their salvation and whose lives—in most cases—centered around the church. Indeed, many of the family members have been ministers and include Baptists (regular), Seventh Day Adventists, Seventh Day Baptists and AME's (African Methodist Episcopal) and there have been various other beliefs.

Mom collected and saved so much family memorabilia—in some ways too much stuff—but the saved news articles, funeral programs and letters help weave the stories. Memorabilia found among Auntie's (Mom's sister, Edna McIntyre) and Cousin Connie's possessions have also added to the stories.

Post 1990s when Marietta wrote most of this, Linda learned more about the family due to a few noteworthy events:

1. In 2004, 1st cousin Donna Crichlow Googled our grandfather's name and discovered volumes of stuff about our grandfather Cyril. She subsequently contacted Dr. Robert Hill, professor and archivist of the Marcus Garvey Archives at UCLA. We all had heard that Cyril had "worked with" Marcus Garvey but never knew the extent of his involvement until this time. Our grandfather had actually been Garvey's resident commissioner in Liberia. More about this in the section on Cyril Crichlow.

2. In 2006 I agreed to help manage the care for Mom's then 92-year-old cousin, Constance Glover Bruce. This required us to clean out her house at 444 Manor Place. Photos and documents there enabled us to learn more about the Glover and Bruce families. Connie's mother, Aunt Goldie Glover Bruce, had purchased the house in 1945 so there was an over-70-year accumulation of letters and memorabilia.

Marietta Stevens ca. 1924

3. In 2010, Auntie (Edna McIntyre) moved to an assisted living facility. In preparing for her move, we found much family memorabilia in the apartment where she had resided for 50 years.

4. A trip to Lynchburg, Virginia, and discussions with Mom and Auntie's cousin Carolyn Brown revealed more information.

5. A trip to Boston and Cape Cod, Massachusetts, and conversations with Cousin Lucy Cromwell provided more information about the Glovers.

6. When we organized Mom's memorabilia, more questions and answers came to light.

With this "new" information, new facts were revealed, so Linda is taking the liberty to add comments to Marietta's manuscript in the sidebars. It is hoped that eventually, other family members will expand upon this information and add their own or their immediate family members' personal recollections.

Most of this manuscript was written by Marietta in the 1990s. Instead of changing the tense, much of the material has been left in the present tense, including the mention of some now deceased people. See the notes section at the end of the book for updates on the narrative. We hope this is not too confusing!

Whenever Mommy tells stories of the past, she usually begins with *Back there, then....*

Linda Crichlow White
2014

Marietta's Introduction

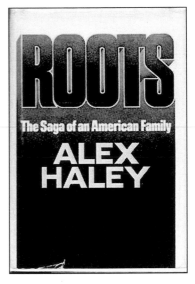

Roots by Alex Haley

Perhaps the most precious resource of any people is their history. A working knowledge of the lives and accomplishments of our ancestors provides us not merely with a look back but a look "in." And through this insight, we are able to attain a greater appreciation of ourselves and our own possibilities.

In order to better understand our present and our future, it is important that we know as much as possible about our past. This process involves reading, research, and talking with those persons who remember events from the past that occurred during their lifetimes, and which, for me, has been a very delayed process—putting it all together in an understandable format.

I have had this family history project in the back of my mind for many years but have let other things get in my way of putting it on paper. I have letters postmarked of more than thirty years ago that I received in reply to my inquiries about the family. I realize now that if I do not get at this task and assemble what information I have gathered, it is likely that it will not get done by me. It would probably be difficult for anyone else to make sense of my notes.

With the help of my computer, of which I have a meager knowledge, I plan to get at least some of my family's history sorted out and recorded. It should shed some light on my forebears and some of it might be interesting to the younger ones coming along.

Tracing the history of any Afro-American family prior to the freeing of the slaves in America is difficult. Some determined and conscientious writers have spent months and probably years searching their family history, as did Alex Haley who traveled to Africa and talked with the griots there to obtain information for his excellent book, *Roots*. Griots were African storytellers who remembered the stories of the family histories of the tribes. The television production of *Roots* in 1977 was the most-watched program at that time. I had the privilege of working with Alex Haley's sister-in-law, Doris Haley, at Sharpe Health School. She taught English there.

I have been able to gather pictures and bits of information of my ancestors who lived in the late 1800s but little or noth-

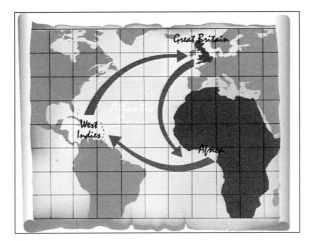

Triangle Trade

New York African Free School No. 2, an institution founded by members of the New York Manumission Society 1787, to provide education to children of slaves and free people of color.

Linda's recent research has revealed that, up until about 1850, the folks now known as Black or African Americans proudly referred to themselves as "Africans." For example, the African Methodist Episcopal (AME) was founded in Philadelphia in 1794. In Boston and in New York City, there were "African Free Schools." Historians have also begun using the term enslaved rather than slaves.

ing of what occurred in the family during slavery. We have been told that wave after wave of immigrants stepped onto the shores of America in the early 1600s. History books tell us that the first Negro slaves were brought to America and landed at Jamestown, Virginia, in 1619. On the return trip from Africa, the slave traders sometimes stopped and dropped off Africans in the Caribbean Islands. These slaves were often put to work on the sugar plantations. The sugar was made into rum and on the return trip to Africa the traders would pick up the rum. The slaves would then be traded for the rum, often making the Africans drunk before loading them tightly on the ships bringing them to America. This became known as the Triangle Trade.

For Africans, at that time called Negroes, the so-called New World meant not only slavery but also a new climate and scenery, new customs, new language, and a land filled with people of a different color than they knew. African families became broken forever—husbands and wives, parents and children—never to see one another again.

Over the years, much was done by the slave owners to discredit Africans and their history and to wipe out whatever progress Africans had made in the continent. On coming to America, the Negro families were separated from their relatives and sold to different slave owners in various locations. They were treated more like animals than human beings. Many slave owners had children with their female slaves, but disowned the children. For this reason, much of the lineage of Negroes has been mixed up, not recorded, and generally lost. In recent years, the newspapers have reported that DNA samples have proven that President Thomas

Jefferson had children with his slave, Sally Hemings. It was probably a widespread habit during slavery for White slave owners to take advantage of the slaves in any way they saw fit.

During the years that slavery existed in the United States and for a long time afterward, people with African ancestry were called Negroes. White people had a lot of trouble spelling the word with a capital N. Many called the slaves Niggers or Nigras, a demeaning term if Whites said it; sometimes a friendly term if Negroes said it. Queer? Yes, but true. The National Association for the Advancement of Colored People (NAACP) was organized in 1913 and soon many Negroes began to be called "Colored." During the Civil Rights Movement that began in the 1950s and escalated in the 1960s, Stokely Carmichael, one of the young leaders of the movement, coined the term Black Power.

Since then, the word "Blacks" has been favorably and widely used when referring to people whose ancestors were slaves from Africa. Some people, as well as myself have a problem using the word "Black" to describe our race. Due to widespread miscegenation, the majority of Colored people in the United States are not black of color. Most are shades of brown to very light complexions. Some are so fair that to look at them no one would know they had African ancestry. But as the saying goes, "One drop makes you whole." Over the decades, many fair-skinned people crossed over and disowned their Negro ancestry so that they could obtain better treatment and better job opportunities. This practice became known as "passing." Shirlee Taylor Haizlip, the author of the book, *The Sweeter the Juice*, tells about this passing over in an interesting way.

Recently, a Black journalist wrote that he had visited Somalia, Tanzania, and some other areas in present-day Africa. His personal conclusion was that, although the slaves were treated horribly, he was thankful that his ancestors had come over on the boat and were brought to America because the drought and tribal rivalry in those countries at the time of his visit seemed to him to be almost unbearable.

What is your opinion?

Despite the brutality of slavery, there were some "loving" relationships between Whites and Blacks—in both the North and the South. And, some White slave owners left property to their Black offspring. Legend says that HBCU Spelman College for girls was founded by wealthy Whites for their Black offspring.

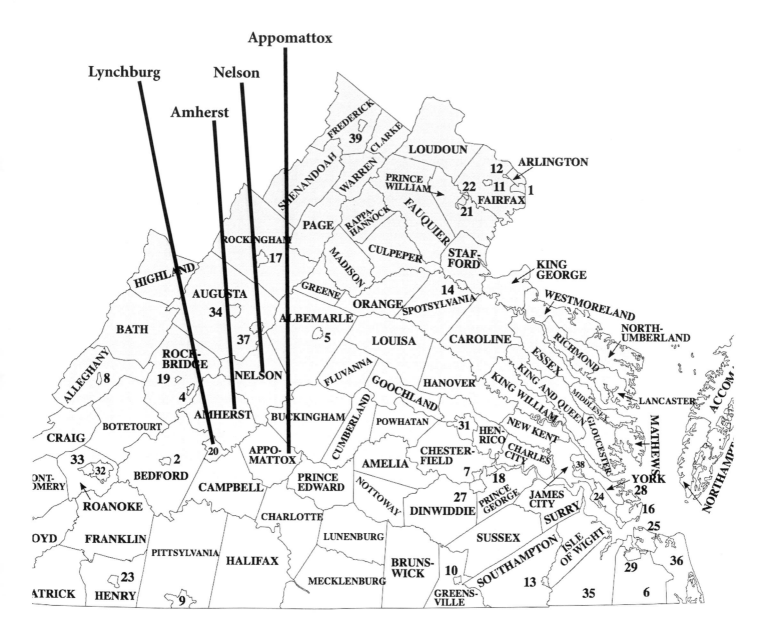

Virginia map showing location of Appomattox, Amherst, Nelson Counties and Lynchburg—locales where Marietta's family originated.

Marietta Stevens Crichlow Direct Lineage

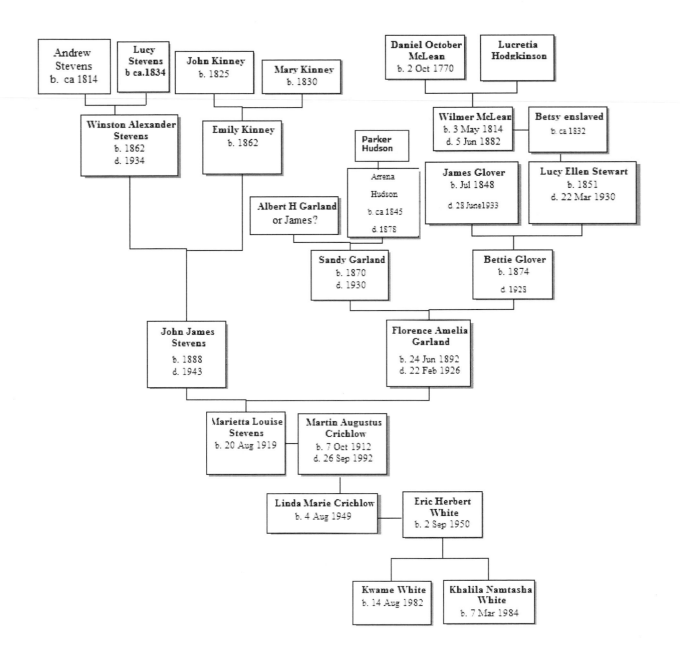

CHAPTER 1
SOUTH CENTRAL VIRGINIA
CIRCA 1870

[This part was written by Linda in May 2014 after obtaining new information about the family. You will learn more about the persons mentioned here in subsequent chapters.]

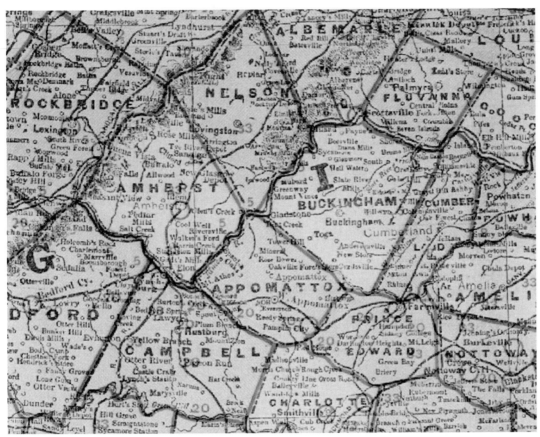

Our ancestors lived in the Virginia counties of Nelson, Appomattox, and Amherst in the mid- to late 1800s.

Marietta's great-grandfather Andrew Stevens lived in the Massies Mill section of Nelson County and his occupation was listed as farming in 1870. Maternal great-great-grandfather Parker Hudson was also listed as a farmer. Farming was what nearly everyone did. Even ancestor Wilmer McLean was listed as a farmer in the Prince William County, Virginia, census of 1860. Tobacco was one of the important crops in these counties and throughout Virginia.

By 1870, some of them were living in Lynchburg, Virginia, having moved from rural to urban like so many others—both Black and Whites—after the Civil War and throughout history. In 1870 Grandmother Lucy Glover lived with her mother

Massies Mill
circa 1880

1

Betsy Stewart, step-father Henry, and siblings on Elm Street in Lynchburg. Betsy is listed as a washer and ironer in the 1870 census. Henry's occupation was listed as "brakeman," a job on the railroad. Some of Betsy's sons and, in other records, some of the Stevenses and Garlands are listed as laborers. This description of laborer from the 1896 book *The College of Life or Practical Self-educator: A Manual of Self-improvement for the Colored Race* helps define the setting:

> As a general laborer, the Negro needs no introduction. He has built the railroads of the South, watered and nurtured its fields, reclaimed its swamps, beautified its cities, and caused the waste places to blossom as the rose.

We see from the *Virginia Slave Births* index that Betsy was in Prince William County in 1860 with children Henry and John, listed as slaves of Wilmer and Virginia McLean. We know from the history books as well as our family oral history that Wilmer McLean moved from Manassas in Prince William County to Appomattox at the start of the Civil War because Wilmer thought he was escaping the violence after the war began "in his front yard." We know that James Glover was born in Appomattox from his death certificate and his 1877 Freedman's Bureau application.

We can presume that the Glovers left Appomattox for Lynchburg at the end of the Civil War, sometime between 1865 and 1870. In 1877, on his application for the Freedman's Bank (where he deposited $10.00), his address (with wife Lucy) is listed as "Canal below Dean's Foundry" which was in Lynchburg.

By 1880, Bessie was listed as a widow in the census. She was still living on Elm Street in Lynchburg and apparently Lucy and James Glover lived next door with their growing family—Bettie, Florence, and Elijah. An article in the *Lynchburg Daily News*, January 21, 1874, reported that husband Henry had been killed in 1874:

> ...a worthy colored man, named Henry Stewart, was caught between the engine and tender and either through carelessness or some inexplicable oversight, was crushed to death.... His remains were placed in a coffin and removed to the residence of his family on the canal, near Sackett's Lumber House. He has been in the employ of the railroad for many years and enjoyed the confidence and respect of his employers, ..was about forty years of age and leaves a wife and several children [not named].

In the 1881 Lynchburg City Directory, James is operating a produce stall on Lynch Street between 19th and 20th.

James and Lucy purchased the house at 1804 Main Street about 1890. When they left Lynchburg to move to Boston, Marietta's maternal grandparents, Sandy and Bettie Garland, purchased the house and raised their children there. After the death of Bettie and Sandy, the house remained in the family as a rental property.

Marietta's paternal grandparents Winston and second wife, Hattie, and family did not move from Nelson County to Lynchburg until about 1887 as they do not show up in the city directories until then. Winston is shown living at 1003 Madison Street in the 1887 City Directory. In 1921, Winston lived at 319 Turnpike Street—later called Florida Avenue and worked as a chauffeur.

Amherst County

Nelson, Amherst, and Appomattox counties were first populated by Native Americans. The Monacan Indians lived in the Amherst area.

In 1761, Amherst County was created from the southern section of Albemarle County and was named for General Jeffery Amherst, the British commander who defeated the French and annexed Canada as a British colony. In 1807, the northern half of Amherst County became Nelson County.

According to Sherrie and William McLeroy, in 1810, 60 percent of households included slaves but most owners held fewer than thirty and most families owned fewer than five. Amherst resident David S. Garland owned 82 slaves.

Amherst County Road, Lynchburg, Va.

The McLeroys point out that there were a number of free Negroes in Amherst and that they generally co-existed peacefully with the Whites, and with the slaves. They even suggest that some Negroes owned slaves although it cannot be determined if they owned them to protect them from being sold to others or if they worked them as slaves. Sandy Garland is listed in the 1870 census as living with his grandfather Parker Hudson. On the 1880 Amherst County agricultural census, Parker Hudson is listed as owning a farm worth $600.00. This is just 15 years after the end of the Civil War so it is POSSIBLE that Parker Hudson was free before the war ended.*

*We are still researching; if anyone else has information about this family, please let us know!

There were many canals throughout Amherst including one that provided public transportation from Lynchburg to Richmond beginning in 1840. There were houses, taverns and boarding houses along the canals in addition to barns for the mules that pulled the boats. By 1865, the canals were being replaced by the railroad. Much labor was needed to build the railroad and no doubt much of that labor was Black. Later, the car came along…and our ancestors traveled many roads.

Appomattox County

Many people today associate the name Appomattox with the "surrender" of the South's General Robert E. Lee to the Union General Ullysses S. Grant on April 9, 1865. However, Appomattox was there much earlier. In 1845, Appomattox County was formed from the surrounding counties of Prince Edward, Charlotte, Buckingham and Campbell. The town was named for the Appomattox River which had

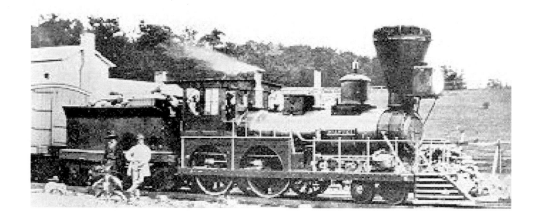

been named after the Appamatuck Indian tribe.

In Virginia, when "court house" is spelled in two words, it indicates a town, the county seat. If it spelled "courthouse" it indicates the physical building. Thus, when people hear that "the surrender" took place at Appomattox Court House, they think it took place in a court building but it was merely the name of the town. The surrender took place in the home of village resident Wilmer McLean who our family believes was the father of—or at least had close ties to—our ancestor Lucy Glover. See appendix for more information on this.

Family stories report that Betsy was the cook for the McLean family and that Lucy was large enough to help out setting the table and such. She is said to have described playing with the McLean children and generally being treated like one of the family. With her long curls, she might have looked like a sister of the McLean daughters. Elson writes that in Lynchburg, there were many mulattos,

There is a marker for a Glover's Grocery Store in Appomattox Historical Park. We can only speculate as to whether or not there was a connection between James Glover and Glover's Grocery Store. Indeed, James later ran a produce stand, worked as a huckster and had a grocery store near his home in Boston.

Nelson County

Nelson County was formed from Amherst in 1807. It is separated from the City of Lynchburg in Campbell County by the James River. The western boundaries of both Amherst and Nelson are the Blue Ridge Mountains, now in the George Washington National Forest. Appomattox County is on the east and Campbell and Bedford on the south. The Piney River and the Tye River divide Amherst County from Nelson. Marietta's paternal ancestors lived in Massie's Mill, Nelson County. The Mill no doubt benefited from the water power of the rivers. There also was much tobacco farming as well as other crops. Census records report that most of the Stevenses were farmers. Some were probably watermen.

In *Four Families of Amherst and Nelson Counties, Virginia*, it is stated that some

COUNTY BRIDGE OVER TYE RIVER. MASSIES MILL, VA.

of the early settlers of Nelson County included the families of Campbell, Massie and Stevens. We have not yet confirmed any relation of our Stevens family to the early settlers but there is probably a link. In the 1870 and 1880 census records, the White and Black Stevenses all lived in the same community.

We have a deed for a real estate transaction from 1910 where it appears that Winston Stevens and wife Emma purchased a piece of property at auction for $300 then soon after sold it for $600.00.

Lynchburg

Known as the Hill City or The City of Seven Hills, Lynchburg was named for its founder, John Lynch, who at the age of 17 started a ferry service across the James River in 1757. He was also responsible for building Lynchburg's first bridge across the river, which replaced the ferry in 1812.

Each of the hills has a name. White Rock Hill was named for the beautiful white rocks one could see on the drive up to the hill. Sandy Garland was a pastor at White Rock Baptist Church. Franklin Hill was possibly named for Benjamin Franklin, a frequent visitor to the area. Diamond Hill was perhaps named for the lots on the turnpike that were triangular shaped. Federal Hill could have been named for the Federalist party that was very influential in the early years of Lynchburg's development. College Hill was named for the military college sponsored by the Methodist Protestants from 1858 until the time of the Civil War. Garland Hill was named for the Garland family including a Samuel Garland, that lived there for more than 100 years. Daniel's Hill was named for Judge William Daniel who owned and subsequently sold most of the land on the hill. There had also been many Garlands in Amherst; perhaps our family is connected to them.

Lynchburg was, according to Steve Tripp, by the 1850s, the second-wealthiest city per capita in the United States. The economy was dependent on tobacco and commerce.

In the later 1800s and early 1900s, Lynchburg was a manufacturing town with companies such as Lynchburg Foundry and Machine Works, Lynchburg Cotton Mill and Craddock-Terry Shoe Co. At least one of our relatives, Bertha Johnson Gilbert, worked at the Hosiery Mill in the 1950's.

In 1859, after John Brown's raid at Harper's Ferry, white Virginians became somewhat so but not overly afraid of slave uprisings. However, it is reported that they did arm themselves and Blacks and Whites continued to live in relative harmony even once the Civil War began in 1861. They still had many faithful enslaved persons. There was a brief skirmish at Lynchburg.

James Elson reports in "Lynchburg on the eve of the War Between the States," that Lynchburg's economy continued to prosper well into the 1860's. On April 1861, the Virginia convention voted 88 for and 45 against secession. As the war progressed and Virginia was part of the confederacy, they suffered in many of the same ways that the rest of the confederacy did and were asked to sacrifice much.

After the Emancipation Proclamation, many Blacks joined the Union Army or the U.S. Colored Troops. It has been reported that ancestor James Glover ran away and served as a water boy during the war. We are still investigating to see if others in our family served in the Civil War.

After the Civil War, a Mennonite named Jacob Yoder came to Lynchburg and operated the first Freedmen's Bureau Schools. Yoder later became superintendent of Lynchburg's colored schools and a revered leader.

Jacob Yoder, a colleague, and some of their pupils are pictured here. The 1870 and 1880 census listed the children of Lucy Glover's mother Betsy Stewart (Lucy's younger siblings) as "attending school." Perhaps they attended Jacob Yoder's school.

Later. Rev. Sandy and Bettie Glover's children (except Florence who attended high school in Boston) attended the Lynchburg Colored High School, later called the Jackson Street School. We will one day search Lynchburg's old school records to try to determine where they attended elementary school.

Most of the Glovers left Lynchburg in 1901. Beginning in about 1910, the Stevenses and most of the Garland children left Lynchburg for warmer suns—places like Duquesne, Pennsylvania and Washington, DC. Mildred Garland Brown's daughters Carolyn and Edwina stayed in Lynchburg and have helped tell this story.h

It is believed that Rev. Sandy Garland helped to organize the Virginia Seminary at Lynchburg. One of our ancestors (Betsy's grandson and Lucy's nephew) Professor Henry Stewart is at the top center in this photo of some of the Seminary's faculty before 1920.

A 1906 notebook entry—in the possession of Carolyn Garland Brown demonstrates that the Garlands and others were diligently trying to uplift the masses of the people:

Minutes of 1st meeting: April Wed 11th 1906
The committee appointed by the womans missionary and educational society Sunday evening April 8th 1906 met at the residence of Mrs. Grace Cummings to devise plans whereby they might arouse the sleeping masses of our city to a sense of duty and necessity of better and more useful lives. This was in reality a consultation meeting for many suggestions followed and many plans presented. Mrs. Rev. Garland was chosen Secretary.

CHAPTER 2

My Paternal Ancestry

So far, I, Marietta Louise Stevens (Crichlow), have been able to trace my father's family back to his paternal great-grandmother. Her name was Harriet. She was born a slave on a plantation somewhere in Nelson County, Virginia, not far from Lynchburg, Virginia. One of her children was named Andrew Stevens. Andrew's wife was listed as Lucy Stevens in the 1870 Census and on his son Winston's marriage license in 1879. Many slaves born before emancipation were not given last names but assumed their master's last name after emancipation.

Andrew and Lucy had nine children: Ida Stevens (Brown), Lizzie Stevens (Welles), Jane Stevens (Gilbert), Betty Stevens, Samuel Stevens, Winston Alexander Stevens, Robert Stevens, Andrew Stevens, Jr., and James Stevens.

The Emancipation Proclamation that was issued by President Lincoln on January 1, 1865, freed the slaves in the states that had seceded and had not returned to the Union. The 13th Amendment, that legally abolished slavery in all of the States, became law on December 18, 1865. However, the descendants of slaves are still struggling with the effects of slavery on the Black race.

THE STEVENS FAMILY

Winston Alexander Stevens, My Paternal Grandfather

Winston Alexander Stevens, one of Andrew and Lucy's children, married Emily Kinney. Winston and Emily were my paternal grandparents. Their ten children were: George Stevens, Ida Lee Stevens (Johnson), John James Stevens (my father), William (Bill) Stevens, Sadie Stevens (Blair), Mamie Stevens, Otelia Stevens, Marie Stevens, Winston Stevens, Jr., and Louis Earl Stevens.

Winston Alexander Stevens, Sr., was my paternal grandfather. He was born in Nelson County, Virginia. I remember seeing him only once when my parents took me with them for a visit to Lynchburg, Virginia. I was about four or five years old. My father was the third child of Winston and Emily. I do not know when Winston moved to Lynchburg from Nelson County, Virginia, but he and Emily bought a home at 319 Florida Avenue, formerly called Turnpike Street, in Lynchburg sometime between 1900 and 1910.

I know very little about Emily Kinney Stevens, who died in 1911. Later, Winston remarried. His second wife was named Hattie. Winston worked for many years at DeWitt's Farm in the Rivermont section of Lynchburg, Virginia. He did farming chores such as packing fruit and helping to raise vegetables. He also delivered

Winston Alexander Stevens

The Stevens family owned and resided at 319 Florida Avenue for at least two generations.

Henrietta Stevens

mail in Nelson County. For many years, he was a member of White Rock Baptist Church located on Florida Avenue in Lynchburg, near his home and served as superintendent of the Sunday school at that church.

Winston lived at 319 Florida Avenue until his death, on February 7, 1934. He died from cardiac renal disease. He probably was about 75 years old at that time, even though his death certificate states that he was "about 65 years old." After his passing, his daughter-in-law, Lula Clemmons Stevens, my Uncle George's widow, took Hattie to live with her at 315 Florida Avenue. Hattie was living with Aunt Lula when she passed.

I did meet some of my paternal great-uncle's children—Ida, Jane and Lizzie, who were Andrew Stevens' children. Ida Stevens (Brown) lived in Connellsville, Pennsylvania, a suburb of Pittsburgh. Jane also lived in suburban Pittsburgh. Lizzie Stevens (Welles) lived in Washington, DC, with her daughter, Mary, in the fifteen hundred block of Fifth Street, NW. During the 1940s I visited her there. How I wish that I had asked for her help in tracing the family's history. Lizzie was in her nineties when she passed. Her daughter, Mary, died about 1960 when she was about ninety years old. Mary had a daughter whose name was Virginia.

My paternal great uncle Robert married a lady named Maggie Turner. They had four children: Earnest, Emmet, Willie and Edward. I never met Willie. Earnest, Edward, and Emmet lived in the Washington, DC, area. Edward was the youngest of the four boys. He married a very nice lady named Desarene. They had three children: Edward Jr., who lives in the state of Washington; Desarene, named after her mother and nicknamed Sandra, lives in Capitol Heights, Maryland; Gilbert lives in Washington, DC. Their mother, Edward's widow, lives at 1624 Lang Place, NE, Washington, DC. Edward, Sr., was born on May 2, 1917, and died in 1976.

10

At one time, he had been pastor of Shiloh Baptist Church in Alexandria, Virginia. Earnest died on May 9, 1996, at the age of ninety-eight. [Desarene passed away in September 2010.]

As I write this in 2001, Emmet is 100 years old and resides at the J.B. Johnson Nursing Center in North East Washington, DC. He seems to be getting along quite well. He can read without eyeglasses and does not need a cane or support to walk around. His mind is quite sharp, too.

Emily Kinney Stevens, my paternal grandmother

My paternal grandmother's name was Emily Kinney before she married Winston Alexander Stevens. Emily's mother's name was Mary. Mary married a man named Norris. They had a son named William Norris and four daughters: Frankie, Lue, Viola, and Ida. After the death of Norris, Mary married John Kinney. John had been married before. One of his children by his first wife, was named Mary Etta Kinney. My parents named me after my father's half-aunt, Emily's half-sister.

Gold pin left to Marietta by her great aunt Mary Etta Kinney in 1926.

I remember Aunt Mary. She used to visit us when I was a little girl. She probably lived with my parents at one time because I have a card dated 1916 from my Aunt Marie, addressed to my great Aunt Mary, at 2024 Fourth Street, NW, Washington, DC, which was my parent's home. She worked for a lady who was employed by the President of the United States. In those days, to have a job working for a well-to-do White family was considered a pretty good job. Aunt Mary lived in the Georgetown section of Washington, DC, and was a staunch member of Nineteenth Street Baptist Church. She died about 1927. In her will, she left some of her money to the church. She also left me a little gold pin, shaped like a bow, with a little diamond in the middle. It is still one of my favorite keepsakes.

Mary Kinney lived at 924 24th Street, NW, in what is now Foggy Bottom. The Jefferson House apartment building stands there now. See Appendix for copy of Aunt Mary's will.

Emily lived at 319 Florida Avenue, Lynchburg, Virginia, with her husband, Winston. She was a busy housewife, raising her large family, until she died in 1911.

My father was John James Stevens, the 3rd oldest.

Children of Winston Alexander Stevens—my paternal aunts and uncles

George was the oldest. He lived in Lynchburg, Virginia, at 315 Florida Avenue. According to some records, he bought this property from my mother's parents, Rev. Sandy and Mrs. Bettie Garland. George married Lula Clemons. They had no children. He had a grocery store and she worked in the insurance business. George died in December of 1925. Aunt Lula continued to live on Florida Avenue taking care of George's stepmother and staying close to the family.

George Stevens

George's sister Ida who helped raise me, had a daughter, Elizabeth Johnson Lee. When Aunt Lula was quite old, Elizabeth (we call her Sis), brought Aunt Lula to

Linda: There are many Stevens families recorded in Nelson County--major land-owners and tobacco farmers going back to the 1600's. There is a Stevens Cove town very close to our ancestors' home of Lovingston. There is very likely a connection.

live with her in Washington, DC. Aunt Lula was up into her 90s when she passed away. She is buried in Luray, Virginia, in the Mount Carmel Church cemetery burial lot. I remember that Aunt Lula's mother, Mrs. Clemons, came to Pennsylvania to visit while I lived there. She was a nice old lady and smoked a corn cob pipe. Aunt Lula also had a brother, John Clemons, who preceded her in death.

Ida was the second oldest of my father's sisters and brothers. She lived in Lynchburg and was left with the responsibility of taking care of the younger siblings after her mother, Emily, died in 1911. On June 17, 1909, she married the Rev. William Preston Johnson (Uncle Willie) from Schuyler, Virginia. They had five children: George, Elizabeth, Emmet, Albert and Bertha.

Ida, along with the other Stevenses, was originally from the Lynchburg, Virginia, area—Nelson County.

Ida and Willie lived for a while in West Virginia where some of their children were born. They later moved to a mining town, Elizabeth, Pennsylvania, where Uncle Willie, as I called him, worked in the mines, and traveled in the southwestern part of Pennsylvania preaching. They were living in Elizabeth, Pennsylvania, when Aunt Ida brought my sister Edna and me from Washington, DC, in 1927 to take care of us there after our mother died. By the time school started, the family had moved to Duquesne, Pennsylvania, a steel mill town about 13 miles southwest of Pittsburgh. (More later about my move to Pennsylvania.)

These following paragraphs refer to Ida and Willie's children. Edna and I grew up with them and we were all raised as sisters and brothers.

George married a girl named Rosabell McClarin. They had no children.

Aunt Ida and Uncle Willie, about 1950

Edna and Mr. McIntyre and cousin Bertha and Aunt Ida beside the house at 111 Jewell Street in Duquesne, ca. 1940

12

Elizabeth married James Clyde Lee. They had four boys: James Clyde, Jr.; Orlando; Kenneth; and Granville. Both James Clydes were called by their middle name, Clyde.

Emmet married Ann Minor and they lived in Pittsburgh. They raised two foster children and adopted one child named Bonnie.

Albert married Lillian Stanback who died during childbirth when their daughter, Barbara, was born in 1943. About 1948 he married Minerva Coles. Together, Albert and Minerva had four beautiful daughters.

Bertha married twice. Her first husband was a soldier, Albert T. Hubb. Her second husband was William "Chick" Gilbert, whom she married in about 1960. Chick had children by his first wife, none by Bertha.

After most of the children had left home, Aunt Ida, Uncle Willie, and Bertha then moved to Braddock, Pennsylvania, for a while, and after World War II ended, they moved to Lynchburg, Virginia, and lived in the family home at 319 Florida Avenue, next door to the White Rock Baptist Church. This house had been purchased by Winston and Emily Stevens and was the house where their children had grown up. Aunt Ida died in September 1954, of a heart problem. Uncle Willie died about 1958.

Albert and daughter Barbara, ca. 1945

Elizabeth and Emmet

PHONE 845-0563

Gilbert's Beauty Salon

MRS. BERTHA J. GILBERT, R. C.
PROP.

COMPLETE BEAUTY SERVICES
AND
MODELS OWN CREATIONS IN
HAND MADE KNITS

805 TAYLOR STREET
LYNCHBURG, VIRGINIA 24504

Aunt Bertha had a beauty salon in Lynchburg and was known for creating beautiful knit fashions.

George Johnson

Seated: Albert's wife Minerva Johnson.
Their children, l-r Debbie, Alisa, Tracy, Barbara, Cecelia

More of Winston and Emily Stevens' children—
Marietta's paternal aunts and uncles

Aunt Sadie married Earl Blair and they lived in Braddock, Pennsylvania, on a very steep inclined street at 1009 Earl Street. They had three boys and a girl—Marion, Joseph, Harold, and Donald.

Marion married a man named Earnest Stanton. They had two children, Earnestine and Earl, and lived at 1320 Penn Avenue, Pittsburgh, Pennsylvania. Earnestine has not yet married. Earl married Karen and they have one child, Jennifer.

William (Bill) married a White lady named Ophelia. I do not know anything about her family. Uncle Bill and Ophelia lived in the Georgetown section of Washington, DC. Back there, then, Georgetown was populated mostly by Colored people. The area was nicknamed Foggy Bottom.

The Blair cousins, Harold, Marion, Joseph in about 1990.

They did not have any children. I do not remember Uncle Bill and Aunt Ophelia visiting us at our home. I remember my parents taking us to visit them once. After Uncle Bill died about 1934, his wife returned to Virginia. I have no photos of them.

It was about 1946 that the White people began buying up property in Georgetown and the Colored residents there were encouraged to sell and/or move. A few Colored people held on to their property, however. From the late 1940s to the present time, Georgetown has been populated by almost all White residents and the value of the property has increased tremendously.

Linda: Before television was invented people did a lot of visiting— pop calling. This was a form of recreation as well as keeping up with friends and relatives.

Mamie had a daughter named Lillian Garland. Lillie's father was named Otis Garland. Mamie died August 24, 1925, at age 24. Aunt Ida kept Lillian (Lillie) with her until she was about 14 years old. She then went to live with Aunt Sadie in Braddock, Pennsylvania. Lillie married three times but had no children. She was divorced from her first husband, Theotris Clements, and later married Thomas Morton. Thomas lost his vision and Lillian took care of him until he passed.

Later she married George Willoughby, a deacon of a church in Pittsburgh. Mr. Willoughby died in1990. Lillie is now in the Forbes Health and Nursing Center in Pittsburgh. She seems to have something similar to Alzheimer's disease.

Otelia Helms ("Aunt Teva"), my father's sister, had a son named Rudolph. Otelia became ill and Aunt Ida had her come to Duquesne, Pennsylvania, to stay with her for a while before Otelia entered a sanitarium where she passed away about 1930.

Aunt Marie, ca. 1965

Marie never married. She left Lynchburg in her teens to work at The Homestead in Hot Springs, Virginia. The Homestead is a luxury resort at the foot of the Allegheny Mountains. The closest major city is Roanoke. Originally built in 1766 as a lodge, it was rebuilt after 1901 and has hosted vacationers ever since, including many diplomats and U.S. presidents. She worked there for several decades in the laundry and also helped take care of a wealthy family's invalid daughter. She returned to Lynchburg, Virginia, after she became elderly and a bit senile. She resided at a nursing home in Amherst, Virginia, where she died about 1973.

Winston never married. He lived with his sister, my Aunt Ida, in Duquesne. He worked at the Carnegie Steel Mill in Duquesne. After Aunt Ida and her family moved to Braddock, Pennsylvania, about 1946, Winston went with them. He died from a fall from a horse about 1948.

Louis lived in North Versailles, Pennsylvania, a suburb of Pittsburgh. He served in the U. S. Navy during World War II and retired from the Edgar Thompson Works in Braddock, Pennsylvania. Louis married Mary Smith. They had no children. After 55 years of marriage, they died within a few days of each other. Louis died on July 24, 1989, on the day his wife was buried.

My Father, John James Stevens

My father, John James Stevens was born on March 12, 1888, in Nelson County, Virginia. The family moved to Lynchburg, Virginia, when he was a youth. His parents had purchased a home at 319 Florida Avenue. Daddy attended schools in Lynchburg, and as it was with most Negroes back there, then, the children had to stop school to help support the family. My father finished the eighth grade before going to work. He worked at Bennie's Hotel in Lynchburg, near Twelfth and Main streets. His boss' name was Thomas Ryan.

When he was in his late teens, Daddy came to Washington, DC, perhaps, because of encouragement by some Lynchburg friends, like a man named Hubbard, who had come to Washington and had obtained fairly decent jobs. My father began to

John James Stevens ca. 1910

John Stevens working on Photostat machine at The Library of Congress about 1926. These machines were the precursors of the Xerox copier!

2024 Fourth Street ca. 1943. The two ladies on the right appear to be Marietta and Edna. Other two unknown.

work as a redcap at Union Station as a parcel porter, which was considered a pretty good steady job for Negroes at that time. Redcaps wore uniforms with red caps and helped travelers with their luggage and boarding the trains.

When he first came to Washington about 1909, John Stevens lived at 1207 Ninth Street, NW. A postal card from his future wife, my mother, was mailed to him at that address in August of 1909. Later he stayed with a family at 935 Fourth Street, NW. This is the address where he and my mother lived when they were first married. This house is located near Mount Carmel Baptist Church, 901 Third Street, NW, where I have been a member since 1937.

In a letter from Boston, Massachusetts, dated April 3, 1912, from Florence Garland to John Stevens when he was living at 935 Fourth Street, NW, she wrote that she "heard he had a new car." This, no doubt, was unusual because most people did not own automobiles at that time and the first Ford car was not made until 1903.

2024 Fourth Street ca. 1999 As of 2013, this property is still in our family and is rented out. Notice how the tree had grown. If only that tree could talk!

My father and mother had kept in touch with each other after Daddy left Lynchburg. Her parents had sent her to Boston to live with her maternal grandparents. My mother came to Washington from Boston in 1912. She and my father were married on August 14, 1912, at 503 D Street, NW, in Washington by the Reverend W. Westray who lived at 1102 Delaware Avenue, SW. At the time of their wedding, my father was twenty-three years old and my mother was twenty years old. The ceremony was witnessed by Alice Martin and Edward Hughes whose names I am not familiar with.

An undated postal card mailed to Florence Garland Stevens from her father in Lynchburg, mentioned her recent marriage. The card was addressed to 935 Fourth Street, NW. The couple apparently did not live at this address very long because they purchased a house at 2024 Fourth Street, NW, in 1913. The house was bought from developer Harry A. Kite. It was listed as being located on Lot 56, Square 2080, in an area that property records called Effingham Place, a part of Ledroit

Park just south of Howard University. Back there, then it was considered the "garden spot of Washington" for Negroes.

The former mayor of Washington, DC, Walter Washington, has lived for many years at 408 T. Street, NW, two blocks down the street from 2024 Fourth Street. The house he lived in was his wife's family home.

Historical records relate that at one time around the year 1900, Negroes were not allowed to live north of Florida Avenue, NW. But things were changing. I remember reading of a riot between Whites and Blacks in that area about 1919.

Many thanks to those brave folks who had the nerve to fight for the rights of all the Negro people.

My father was a hard and steady worker outside of the home. Even during the Great Depression that began in 1929 when many people were unemployed, fortunately, he was never without a job. In addition to his day job as a redcap, he worked at night at the Wardman Park Hotel, 2600 Woodley Road, NW, now the Sheraton-Washington Hotel.

The
Monitor Shoe
$5.50

ASCOT LAST.

Lace, in Black Colonial Calf, calf lined, double sole.
Lace, in Black Colonial Calf, cloth lined, double sole.
Lace, in Russet Colonial Calf, cloth lined, double sole.
Russet Colonial Calf, Blucher, cloth lined, double sole.
Made with cork innersole.
Colonial Calf will not crack.

The United States entered World War I on April 6, 1917. My father was required to register for military service as were all the men about his age. He was about twenty-nine years old at that time. He was not classified at the top of the eligible list to serve in the war because he and my mother had a new baby girl. The war ended formally on November 11, 1918, when Germany signed the Armistice.

My mother and father had three children. A son, John James Stevens, Jr., was born on August 29, 1915. He lived about 8 hours before he died. He was buried in Payne Cemetery. Edna Hortense was born on May 22, 1917. I, Marietta, (birth certificate spells it Mary Etta) was born August 20, 1919.

About 1922, Daddy began to work as a photostat operator in the photo-duplicating laboratory at the Library of Congress. The Library of Congress is located at First and Independence Avenue, SE, close to the U.S. Capitol. This was considered a good position for a Negro back then because most Negroes were hired only as laborers.

His work involved making copies and preparing material requested by U. S. Congressmen. It required a good bit of skill on the machines that were used at that time. He worked Monday to Friday and one-half day on Saturday. Then, on Sunday he went back to the Library of Congress (sometime called the Congressional Library) where he worked from 2:00 to 10:00 p.m. as an admissions agent at the door of the Library Reading Room.

I remember my mother taking my sister and me to visit the Library. We would get all dressed up in our Sunday best clothes, little gloves and hats. I thought the Library was just so beautiful and spacious. We would go up to the balcony and look down over the Reading Room area where my father would be working and checking in the visitors, directing them to the proper places in the Reading Room, and clicking a hand-held instrument that counted each visitor that entered the Room. I had no idea that several years later I would spend hours at the Library of Congress, sometimes not willingly, working on research papers for my classes at Howard University.

About 1924, Daddy became ill with double pneumonia. He evidently was quite sick, and doctors did not have very good methods then to treat the disease. But he recovered nicely. The doctor told him that to stay healthy he should swallow two whole raw eggs for breakfast every day. From that time on for the rest of his life, every single day, that was part of his breakfast, along with a glass of fruit juice and a cup of coffee. He never, as far as I know, ate cereal or cooked eggs, or sausage, or bacon. He tried to follow the doctor's orders; at least to that extent. Now, doctors say too many eggs can cause high cholesterol levels. Little or nothing was known about cholesterol in 1924.

Daddy was a member of the Odd Fellows Lodge and attended meetings from time to time. I do not remember that he attended church very much. Most of his time was spent working and supporting the family. He did enjoy playing checkers. There was a barber shop across the street from our house on Fourth Street, NW. When he had time, he would go over there and play checkers. He also would go to the drug store at the northeast corner of Fourth and Elm Streets and chat with the Colored pharmacist, Dr. Luther Wiseman, and they would sometimes play a game of checkers. Daddy's friends called him "Steve." Quite a few folks called him "J. J."

Daddy continued to wear "high-topped" laced shoes for the rest of his life, long after they had gone out of style. He always wore a shirt and tie. I do not remember having seen him dressed any other way. Even if he took a nap, he would keep on his shirt and tie. His work habits had become ingrained and that was the way he dressed for work every day. He was truly a conscientious worker. He almost never took a day off from work and almost never took a vacation.

After my mother died in 1926, Daddy tried to find help to take care of my sister and me. In August 1927, his sister Ida came from Pennsylvania and took us to live with her. Daddy stayed in Washington. He kept a room in the house for himself and rented the rest of the house. He continued to work at the Library of Congress and came to Pennsylvania to visit us from time to time. He never remarried.

Freedmen's Hospital

I returned to Washington in 1937 to attend Howard University. In the summer of 1938 Daddy and I refurbished the house and I kept house for the two of us. A married couple rented one of the rooms. Edna, my older sister, returned to DC in 1942 to take a government job and stayed with us.

About January 1943, Daddy had a mild stroke. He had a nose bleed one night and the next morning he said he felt weak. He continued ailing and in May, much to his regret, he retired on disability from his job at the Library of Congress. He became weaker and in November of 1943 he reluctantly went to be admitted as a patient at Freedmen's Hospital. This was a few blocks down the street from our house, in the building where the television station of Howard University is now located.

He had become quite thin, never having weighed much over 145 pounds. He was about five feet seven inches tall. On November 23, 1943, he passed away at Freedmen's Hospital at the age of fifty-four. The doctor who had first attended him was Dr. George Bullock, the son of Reverend Bullock, the prominent pastor at Third Street Baptist Church. Rev. Bullock was the father-in-law of the future mayor of DC, Walter Washington. About November 15, 1943, Dr. Bullock was killed in an automobile accident while riding with friends on Benning Road, NE. Dr. Bullock was about 40 years old and had set up his office in his father's home at 408 T Street, NW. No one thought that he would pass away before my father.

Daddy's funeral was held at Frazier's Funeral Home, Fourth and Florida Avenue, NW, and Rev. Moses Beasley preached the eulogy. Aunt Ida and Aunt Sadie came to the funeral from Pennsylvania. He was buried at Harmony Cemetery, which was located on Rhode Island Avenue, NE, near 10th Street. About 1965, when plans for the subway at 10th Street got underway, the cemetery was moved to 7101 Sheriff Road, Landover, Maryland. His remains were transferred to the McCoy Section, Lot 80, Grave No. 6.

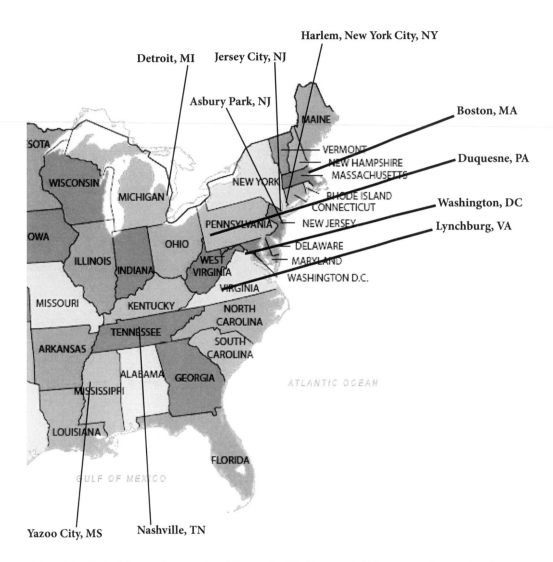

Map of the United States, showing Lynchburg, VA; Washington, DC; Duquesne, Pennsylvania; and Boston, Massachusetts—locales where most of Marietta's family are associated. When you read about Marietta's husband in Chapter 7, you will see that Martin Crichlow and his family lived many places as Martin's parents traveled as missionaries—first for the Seventh Day Adventist Church and later for the Seventh Day Baptist Church. Martin was born in Yazoo City, Mississippi. They also lived in Nashville, Tennessee; Detroit, MI; Jersey City and Asbury Park in New Jersey, and Harlem in New York City. After the family moved to Washington, DC, about 1927, they lived in several different homes there.

MY MATERNAL ANCESTRY, THE GLOVERS

JAMES A. GLOVER: MY MATERNAL GREAT-GRANDFATHER

I have not yet been able to trace any of the ancestors of my maternal great grandfather. However, my great-grandfather's name was James A. Glover. Family information states that he was born to the slave master and a slave woman.

He was born on July 28, 1847, in Appomattox County, Virginia. There are no records available of the names of his parents or of his brothers and sisters. On his death certificate his parents are listed as "unknown." At Appomattox Court House National Park, there is a sign that says Glover's Store. Perhaps that was owned by some of his (White?) ancestors.

Picture of Glover family from about 1900.
First row (l-r): Goldie, James Glover, Joe Glover, Lucy, James Glover, Jr.
Back row (l-r): Florence, Bettie, Elijah, Carrie, Lawrence.

I have been told that when he was fourteen years old he ran away from his slave owners and served as a "water boy" in the Civil War. In the 1880 census report James was listed as a huckster; he sold vegetables as well as coal and wood. When I was a child, I remember hucksters would come along the streets of Washington, DC, in horse-drawn wagons shouting the names of the products they had for sale such as coal, ice, or watermelon. It is likely this is what he did in Virginia.

James married Lucy Ellen Stewart. They had nine children: Bettie Marian (my grandmother), Florence Ervenia, Elijah Eugene, Lawrence E., Carrie, Goldie Myrtie Beatrice, James A. Jr., Joseph and Annie. My mother Florence Garland Stevens was, no doubt, named after her aunt Florence Glover (Scott).

By 1899, the family had purchased a home at 1804 Main Street, Lynchburg, Virginia. They had an oyster and fish business called "James and Lu." The 1804 Main Street house later became the home of Reverend and Mrs. Sandy Asbury Garland, my maternal grandparents.

According to Harry S. Ferguson's book, *The Participation of the Lynchburg Virginia Negro in Politics—1865-1900*, James Glover (Negro) was one of the Republicans nominated from the Third Ward to run for councilman in the election held May 23, 1889. Ferguson also related that "...the Negro Republican candidates were defeated by a narrow margin, due to the split in the Party." On page 33 of the book, the writer further states: "The candidates listed were all property holders and respectful citizens. They occupied vocations ranging from the professions to common laborer. Among the professions, there was a lawyer, Rawling Merchant; a medical doctor, Dr. Buggs and a minister of the gospel, J. W. Calloway. The above vocational classifications indicate that these Negro citizens could meet the requirements of office holders of that period."

James Glover was a deacon at Court Street Baptist Church. When some of the members decided to leave the church and build a new church named Eighth Street Baptist Church, the Glovers joined the Eighth Street Church congregation and became charter members there.

Over the years, some of the Glover children moved to Boston, Massachusetts. During the early 1900s James and Lucy Ellen also moved to Boston. The family lived at 80 Kendall Street in the Roxbury section of Boston. During this time James owned a grocery/restaurant.

On June 28, 1931, James died of acute myocarditis brought on by arteriosclerosis. He was 86 years and 11 months old. He was buried in Glenwood Cemetery. At the time of his death, he resided at 48 Nichols Street, Everett, Massachusetts, which was probably the home of one of his children.

LUCY ELLEN STEWART GLOVER: MY MATERNAL GREAT-GRANDMOTHER

My maternal great-grandmother was Lucy Ellen Stewart Glover. I never had the privilege of meeting, corresponding with, nor talking with her. I have been told that her mother was Betsy Love, a slave of an Irish slave master named McLean. [Since the time that Marietta wrote this, we have confirmed that the "master" was Wilmer McLean, in whose house Robert E. Lee surrendered to General Ulysses S. Grant, ending the Civil War.]

Betsy had two sisters, Fannie and Lynn. Betsy married Henry Stewart and they had six children. Their first child was Lucy Ellen. Lucy had five siblings: Henry Stewart, Jr.,; James Stewart; John Stewart; William Stewart; and Fannie Stewart. According to cousin Carolyn Brown, Henry Stewart, Jr., was the father of music teacher Professor Benjamin Harry Stewart.

Lucy Ellen Stewart was born on August 2, 1851, in or near Manassas, Virginia. I know nothing about her early years. I have been told that she never learned to read or write. At the time that she was growing up, it was against the law in many places to teach Negroes to read and write. After she and James A. Glover were married on October 7, 1869, they purchased a home at 1804 Main Street in Lynchburg, Virginia.

Linda:
According to Lucy's death certificate, her mother's maiden name was Betsy Love. I have been told that she was a slave of Wilmer Mclean and his wife Virginia Hooe Mason McLean. According to family accounts, Betsy was a cook for the family. In the 1870 census, Betsy is listed as Betsy Stewart, wife of Henry Stewart. For more about Betsy and Lucy's connection to the McLeans, see Appendix (A)

Around 1901, she and James moved to Boston, Massachusetts. My mother (Lucy and James' granddaughter), moved from Lynchburg, Virginia, in about 1909 to live with them until she moved to Washington in 1912. Lucy Ellen Stewart Glover died at age 79 on March 22, 1930, of diabetes mellitus brought on by a diabetic coma. She too, was buried at Glenwood Cemetery, Everett, Massachusetts. Her residence at the time of her death was 42 Harvard Street, Everett, Massachusetts.

Professor Benjamin Harry Stewart, who was probably Lucy's nephew, lived in Lynchburg, Virginia. He was very skilled at playing the piano and in that area had an excellent reputation as being the best piano teacher around. He taught my first cousins Edwina and Carolyn piano lessons when they were growing up during the 1930s and 1940s.

[In December 2013, Carolyn clarified, Prof. Benjamin Harry Stewart was the music teacher. His father was Henry Jr. His grandfather was Henry. Carolyn also noted that in a record book that Papa Garland (grandfather) recorded deaths of many citizens, he made this notation: "Mr. Horace Stewart, brother of Mrs. Lucy Glover died Thursday, June 20th, 1918." So there must have been an additional brother.]

☙ PICTURE FRAMES & WINDOW SHADES — Made to order at LOWEST PRICES by MOOSE BROS. & CO., 913 MAIN STREET.

GLA   214   GOL

Glass, Mollie C, wid James, res 1813 Union.
" Richard, c, lab, res 1624 Locust.
GLASS, RICHARD W (R W Glass & Co), res 2110 Grace.
GLASS, ROBERT H JR, business mngr The Lynchburg News and sec and treas Advance Newspaper Co, res 614 Court.
GLASS, R W & CO (Richard W Glass), proprs Otey's Place 1109. (See p 7.)
" Stephen, c, lab, res 1610 18th.
" Sydney T, clk W B Foster, res 910 5th ave.
" W O, barkpr R W Glass, res 2110 Grace.
Glauner, Henry S, carp, res Dearing, Rmt.
" Rosa Miss, clk J R Millner & Co, res Dearing, Rmt.
Gleaves, R Taylor, civil engr, res Rivermont ave.
Glenn, Virginia W, wid William S, res 412 Harrison.
" Walter J, night chief opr W U Tel Co, res 516 Madison.
Glover, Harmon, c, wks Moorman's Warehouse.
" James, c, (J Glover & Son), res 1804 Main.
" J & Son, c (J and L), fish and oysters 613 Main.
" Lawrence J, c, (Glover & Son), res 1804 Main.
" Lucy, c, eating house 613 Main, res 1804 Main. ◄
Gnehm, John U, grocer 1343 Main.
GODDIN, H TAYLOR, mngr R G Dun & Co, res 611 Madison.
Goff, Creed W, cigar mkr, res 1305 Buchanan.
" Edward C, wks Lg Elec Co, res 1219 Buchanan.
" Edward W, wks city, res 1219 Buchanan.
" Floyd, c, wks John S Shaner.
GOFF, NATHAN HON, Judge U S Circuit Court, office U S Court House, res Clarksburg, W Va.
" Nathaniel T, wks Cotton Mill, res 1309 Buchanan.
" Sarah E, wid J L, res 1309 Buchanan.
" Wilbur W, butcher Louis P Shaner, res 1309 Buchanan.

This page from the Lynchburg 1900 City Directory indicates that James and Lucy operated an "Eating House" and sold fish and oysters at 613 Main Street.

This is what downtown Lynchburg looked like in the 1920s. Note the Woolworth's store. Woolworth's was a 5 and 10 cents store. There was at least one in every small and large city in the United States. The one in Greensboro, NC became famous when students from North Carolina A & T State College sat in to demand equal rights in 1960, serving as a catalyst for the Civil Rights Movement.

MY MATERNAL GREAT-GRANDPARENT'S CHILDREN

My maternal great-grandparents had nine children: Bettie Marion, Florence Ervenia, Elijah Eugene, Lawrence E., Carrie, Goldie Myrtie Beatrice, James A. Jr., Joseph, and Annie. Most of their children were born in Lynchburg, Virginia, and later they moved to the Boston, Massachusetts, area.

I knew two of my maternal great-grandparent's children: Bettie (my grandmother) and Bettie's youngest sister, Goldie. Goldie was born in 1888. She married Charles Herbert Bruce, Sr. They had three children: Charles Herbert, Jr., Constance Glover Bruce, and Althea Virginia Bruce. Goldie raised her children in Somerville, Massachusetts. She and her husband divorced about 1933. She moved to Washington, DC, and at one time worked as a matron at Slowe Hall, located at Second and T Streets, NW. Back there, then, it was a residence for young Negro "government girls" who came to DC to work during the War. It is now a student residence building for Howard University students. [On the next page is a brief biography of Goldie that was found at Manor Place.]

Goldie and Charles Bruce ca. 1908

Linda: After we started looking after Connie, we learned that her brother Charles was a Harvard graduate Class of 1933. He was a classmate of Frank Snowden, who later became Dean at Howard University. In fact, Connie said the Snowden and Bruce families were friends in Boston.

About 1950, when my mother's sister, (Goldie's niece) Nannie, took me to meet her, she was living at 444 Manor Place, NW. Aunt Goldie had purchased the house in 1945. The neighborhood then was known as Pleasant Plains, but is now part of Columbia Heights. I did not know about her living in Washington prior to that time. Goldie died in 1977 at the age of 89.

Goldie and Charles Bruce's son Charles, Jr., was born in Cambridge, Massachusetts, on October 27, 1911. He married Nan Lynn on November 13, 1937. Nan had two children by a previous marriage—Robyn Lynn and David Lynn. Charles was an engineer and a merchant marine commander. He died at Sag Harbor, Long Island, New York, on January 15, 1989. His ashes were scattered at sea as he requested.

Constance, Goldie and Charles Bruce's middle child, was born in Somerville, Massachusetts, on April 12, 1915. Connie is my maternal grandmother's sister's child. Connie lived in New York for several years before moving to Washington, about 1942, and worked in the Federal government for several years. She lived with her mother and helped take care of her during her mother's final illness.

After her mother passed, Connie continued to live in her mother's home, 444 Manor Place, NW, and still lives there today, not far from my home on Randolph Street. She never married. We have visited often. She is a charming, chatty person and has furnished me with some information about the Glover family. [Connie passed away in July 2012.]

Connie has been a life member of the National Council of Negro Women for many years and regularly attends the annual conferences. I did not know the other members of her family very well. I met her brother and sister only once when they

Constance Glover Bruce

Goldie Glover Bruce
First row (l-r): Aunt Lil, Charles' wife, Charles Jr., Goldie.
Back row (l-r): Constance, Sandy, Althea

Linda: When cleaning out 444 Manor Place in 2006, we discovered several diaries of Aunt Goldie's that described the goings on there. Apparently Althea lived there with Aunt Goldie during most of the 1950s until she and her husband reunited about 1960. Althea worked for many years as an administrative secretary at the World Bank, probably one of the first African Americans to do so. During this time she purchased a Packard (car) that she enjoyed and purchased a little house at Oyster Harbor, Maryland, which she and Aunt Goldie dubbed "The Doll House." She eventually retired to Tucson, Arizona, where her sister-in-law lived. Her death certificate states that she died aboard a cruise ship.

The document on the following page is a biography written by Aunt Goldie in 1943 while she was serving as dorm matron at Slowe Hall. She had been asked by her supervisor to write the bio apparently for a program that was taking place. The document reveals history not only about Aunt Goldie but about all of the Glovers.

were visiting their mother on Manor Place, about 1952.

Althea, the youngest of Goldie and Charles Bruce's children, was born on July 17, 1917, in Somerville, Massachusetts. Althea was married to Reuben Walter Allen, Jr. They had one son, Reuben Walter Allen, III, who presently lives in Napervillle, Illinois, a suburb of Chicago. Althea died in 1987 of a heart problem while traveling on a cruise ship off the coast of Los Angeles, California.

December 30,1943.

STORY OF MY WORK LIFE

Having been born of business parents(James & lucy Glover) in Lynchburg,Va. June 17th.1888 and eighth in a family of ten children, I was very young when I began helping in the Neighborhood grocery store owned by my parents and managed by an older sister.

As soon as I could make change correctly I was allowed to sell and become a real clerk and if I had been especially good, I was allowed to sell fresh vegetables, fish and oysters on the Public Market up town where my father had a stall, or even to go to the "Elite Glover's Restaurant,still farther up town and serve the meals to patrons. There my mother was manager.

In my 12th year,april 1901 my family moved to Boston, Mass. where again I was clerk in their grocery store and also learned to order merchandise, as we handled wood and coal and other things that were not sold in Virginia. This I did before and after school until I was graduated from the Girls'High School in June 1907.West Newton St. Boston.

Now I had the opportunity to spend more time at sewing,which had been a lifelong secret desire. I became an apprentice under the French dressmaker, Mme. Delvine Boulanger and worked with Mme Nana VonDerLuft beginning as plain sewer and remaining as finisher after my three children had grown to School age. I also had a sewing business in my home.

In Sept.1928, I opened a Shoppe of my own in Somerville, Mass where I then had my home, a two family house, renting one apartment. My children were then old enough to need something to do after school, so "GOLDIE"--Sew and Help Sew Shoppe was opened with a Lending Library Greeting Cards and small Micellaneous stock that children could handle with the sewing done in the rear of it. Employed three regular sewers.

In 1935 After my son had been teaching for two years at the Tennessee State College, and one daughter had entered College there, I ventured with the younger daughter to visit to see if I would like to change States. I arrived at the College May 30th1935 on Class Day.

As an assistant was badly need in their Cafeteria I at once went in to help,and when the Registered Nurse left the School without one I was asked to become School Nurse as I had had Red Cross Training in Evening Classes while in Boston,and a practical nurse wasneeded to work with the Doctor. Unknown to the President or the Doctor, I took a correspondence Course in Nursing at the Chicage School of Nursing,and in due time-October 1938 I received my Diploma classifying me as a Trained Practical Nurse. They were very happy.

My interest in the School, however, soon carried me into other Campus work. When I left there in 1941 to take my vacation, I had been School Nurse, Asst. Dean of Women Receptionist to Guests visiting and Transient, also custodian of Campus keys, Furnishings and supplies. Fourteen N.Y.A.students assisted me in any way I needed them from cleaning the Guests quarters to carrying meals to patients. They were selected by their natural ability.

When I reached Boston on my vacation and knew again the reunion of my children I decided to stay, and started nursing in the Massachusetts Phycopathic State Hospital. Nursed there four months. I left there to nurse in a Rest Home for aged Jews under a Mrs. Ada Heller.

In January 1943 I left Mrs Heller to accept Civil Service work in the War Dept in Washington, D.C.I worked in the Tempo X.building 7 months when an involuntary separation gave me 15 days vacation,at which time the Assistant Resident manager of Slowe Hall, my Washington home, was taken il and I went to her rescue and tried to carry on for her. This I am still doing, under the able management of Mr.Spurgeon Burke.

My salaries have grown from 50cents a week from my dad to $2200 which I am now getting.   Yours Truly

Goldie G.Bruce

CHAPTER 3

My Maternal Ancestry,
The Garlands

REVEREND SANDY GARLAND,
MY MATERNAL GRANDFATHER

My maternal grandfather was the Rev. Sandy Asbury Garland. I called him Papa Garland and I remember seeing him three times. First, when I was about four years old, my parents took my sister and me to Lynchburg to visit. Then, when my mother had her final illness in 1926, he and my grandmother came to Washington.

When I was about nine years old Papa Garland came to visit some of his relatives who lived in Braddock, Pennsylvania. This was at the time that I was living with my father's sister Ida, and her family in Duquesne, Pennsylvania, a few miles from Braddock. He came to Duquesne and took Edna and me to visit his nephew Arthur and Arthur's family. This was the last time I saw him or talked with him. Most people did not have phones in their homes at that time. To use a phone, folks went to a store or wherever they could find a place that had one.

Reverend Sandy Asbury Garland died on November 9, 1930, at the age of sixty-seven, of what the doctor called prostatitis. His daughter, my Aunt Mildred, had taken care of him during his final illness. Just prior to his final illness, he was serving as pastor of Peaceful Baptist Church in Lynchburg, Virginia. His eulogy was delivered by Rev. J. W. Tynes, Pastor of Eighth Street Baptist Church in Lynchburg.

Rev. Garland was a Christian gentleman and highly respected among Lynchburg citizens. Edward H. Brown, Aunt Mildred's husband and

Reverend Sandy Garland, wife Betty, and children Florence and Nannie—ca1890.

Rev. S. A. GARLAND, D. D.

Once the Pastor of Brookville Baptist Church,
Campbell County, Va.

Pastored in the City of Lynchburg, Va., twenty-two
years ; now Pastor of Morning Star Baptist Church,
Evergreen, Appomattox County, Va.

Now Pastor at Peaceful Baptist Church, Lynchburg, Va.
Also engaged in Evangelical work.

1804 MAIN STREET, - LYNCHBURG, VA.

Dr. Garland's son-in-law, Edward Brown (husband of Mildred), remembered that Sandy Garland had a great rapport with Lynchburg's Senator Carter Glass. Uncle Edward told how Rev. Garland was invited to Washington, DC, by Senator Glass where they were in consultation regarding plans for Lincoln Cemetery.

According to his obituary, Rev. Garland often took his granddaughter with him as he visited members of his church in homes throughout the city; many of those visits took him into homes of well-to-do citizens where members of the church were employed and "lived on the lot." Visits into many of these homes led him to become acquainted with many individuals throughout the city who were not members of his congregation.

Some of his records indicate that Grandpa Garland was a concerned and active member of the community and was highly regarded among people in the area in which he lived and worked and among others in the organizations of which he was a member. He was an active member of the most Worshipful Grand Lodge of Masons, Prince Hall Affiliate, and was a leader in the Baptist State Convention.

When city officials decided to limit burials in the City Cemetery, Rev. Garland was Vice President of the organization of Baptist churches which sought to purchase a site for a new cemetery. The Lynchburg Baptist Cemetery Association was organized on July 25,1925. Member churches of the Association were Diamond Hill, Eighth Street, White Rock, Mount Carmel, Rivermont, Fifth Street, Dearington, Peaceful Baptist and South Lynchburg Baptist Churches.

In 1890, Rev. Garland conducted the first revival that was held at the Mount Olive Baptist in Amherst, Virginia. An announcement stated that there were ninety-nine converts during the course of that revival. There is a legal document that shows that my maternal grandparents sold a piece of property to George Stevens, who was my father's oldest brother. This transaction took place on December 2, 1913. The property was described as being a lot of ground on Turnpike Street. George Stevens and his wife, Lula Clemons Stevens lived at 315 Turnpike Street (later called Florida Avenue) for the rest of George's life. This house was next door to my paternal grandfather's house (George's father, Winston Stevens, Sr.). Aunt Lula stayed there until about five years before she died, when she then came to Washington, DC, to live with my cousin Elizabeth Johnson Lee and her family.

A brief biography of Sandy Garland in *A History of the Richmond Theological Seminary* says that he completed his studies at the Richmond Institute in 1885 and was president of the Ministerial Union of Lynchburg. Grandpa Garland reported: "If I am any good to the world, it is due to the training that I received in this school. I would have been in obscure life if it had not been for the intellectual training that I received from the Richmond Institute…I have found that there is no royal road to success…that we need not go through the world expecting the trees to bow down."

BETTIE MARIAN GLOVER, MY MATERNAL GRANDMOTHER

My maternal grandmother was named Bettie Marian Glover. She was the first child born to James and Lucy Ellen Glover. Apparently she was born in or near Lynchburg, Virginia, in 1872. Bettie was married to Sandy Asbury Garland at Court Street Baptist Church, Lynchburg, Virginia, on July 15, 1891. This, according to an article published in the newspaper at that time, was a beautiful wedding. Grandma Garland played the piano and was a skilled seamstress. Most young ladies back there, then were taught needlework and cooking.

Bettie and Rev. Sandy A. Garland had six children: Florence Amelia (my mother), Nannie, John Wesley, Sandy Asbury, Jr., Mildred, and Mary who died in infancy. Among the skills Bettie taught her daughters was how to play the piano, how to sew, how to do needlework, and how to cook.

Many children have the enriching experience of having had close contact with their grandparents. I remember having seen my maternal grandmother only twice. The average person did not travel very much when I was a child.

Once, my parents took my sister and me with them to Lynchburg in about 1923 when I was about four years old. I remember the house at 1804 Main Street that was originally owned by Grandma Garland's parents. She and my grandfather probably purchased the house from the Glovers. Over the years, after my grand parents had died, the family, particularly Aunt Mildred, tried to keep the house up to date and in good condition. The house was rented out with Aunt Mildred sending a portion of the rent of two to three dollars a month to each of the "heirs" including Edna and me. It finally was torn down about 1960.

I saw Grandma Garland again in February of 1926 when she and Grandpa Garland came to Washington during my mother's illness. That was the last time I saw her. She became ill herself shortly after she returned to Lynchburg in 1926. She died in 1928 of tuberculosis, a fairly widespread infectious disease at that time and difficult to cure. Back then, throughout the United States, most hospitals had tuberculosis annexes or sanitariums.

Four generations: clockwise from right: sitting, Lucy Stewart Glover, Bettie Glover Garland, Standing: Florence Stevens holding baby Edna Stevens, about 1917

Bettie Glover Garland in front of the family home at 1804 Main Street ca 1918.

GLOVER-GARLAND WEDDING

(from a Lynchburg newspaper clipping, probably the Black newspaper, *The Counselor*)

On Wednesday evening, July 15, (1891), Court Street Baptist Church was the scene of a beautiful marriage. The event being the uniting into matrimonial alliance of Miss Bettie M. Glover and Rev. S. A. Garland, both of this city.

Long before the appointed hour the spacious house was filled to overflowing; the soft light fell gently over all, a thousand fans stirred a gentle breeze and Rev. Morris was delivering good advice to an appreciative audience, when it was made known that the marriage procession was at the door. There was silence for a minute, then came in the ushers walking to the time of a beautiful wedding march, rendered by the accomplished Mrs. T. M. Coles.

Crossing in front of the altar, they faced each his accompanying fellow, and it was a scene of mingled beauty, grandeur and solemnity. They were all in evening dress, tan colored kids* and their shoes were tied with white. Next came the groom accompanied by his best man, Mr. Thos. D. White.

Then, as the music lowered almost to an inaudible key, the bride entered, resting lightly on the arm of her maid of honor, Miss Maggie L. Butler. She was beautifully attired in surah silk, and wore the bridal veil through which shone a beautiful pin which was artistically worked in her hair.

In her hand she carried a beautiful bouquet of cut flowers. Miss Butler was attired in surah silk to match, wore a sweet smile through the whole and acted her part gracefully.

The ushers were Messrs. W. A. Mitchell, S. C. Brown, William White and John W. Henderson.

Rev. Garland is a promising young minister, the pastor of two churches, White Rock Baptist Chapel and Brookville Baptist Church. He is to be congratulated on getting such an able helpmate.

Miss Glover, the daughter of our townsman, Deacon Jas. Glover, is an accomplished young lady, a graduate of our Lynchburg High School, a teacher in Court Street Baptist Sabbath School and an earnest Christian worker.

We wish the happy couple a long and prosperous life. Presents were many, beautiful and varied.

No cards.

---

*Kids refers to the kid(skin) of baby goat which was very fashionable for shoes and gloves in the late 19th and early 20th centuries.

FLORENCE A. M. GARLAND, MY MOTHER

My mother's name was Florence Amelia M. Garland. I do not know what the "M" in her name stood for. She was born in Lynchburg, Virginia, on June 24, 1892, the oldest child of Sandy and Bettie Garland. Her sisters and brothers were Nannie, John, Sandy, Jr., and Mildred.

Grandma Garland had taught her daughters many of the niceties of the day. My mother played the piano, was an expert at sewing and needlework and was a good cook. My Aunt Nannie said she used to make her own coatsuits, as they were called back then. Later, my daughter, Linda sewed all of her clothes. Perhaps it was from my mother that Linda got her talent for sewing. Linda is an expert at it!

Mama attended school in Lynchburg until 1909. The following school year, her parents sent her to Boston, Massachusetts, to live with her grandparents, James and Lucy Ellen Stewart Glover. Uncle Sandy told me they felt that she would receive a better education there. On June 5, 1911, she graduated from the Girls' High School in Boston.

She had kept up her correspondence with her family and friends in Lynchburg during her stay in Boston. A card postmarked December 14, 1909, and addressed to Florence Garland at 1804 Main Street, Lynchburg, shows that she apparently had not yet gone to Boston. The card was sent to her from John Stevens who then lived in Washington and was staying at 1207 Ninth Street, NW. He and his family had lived on Florida Avenue, in Lynchburg, a few blocks up the hill from the Garland family.

After leaving Lynchburg, my mother and father continued to keep in touch. My mother probably had not visited Washington before the summer of 1912. On the 14th day of August in 1912 John Stevens and Florence Garland were married by the Rev. Westray at 503 D Street, NW. They probably stayed at 935 Fourth Street, NW, for a short time before purchasing a home at 2024 Fourth Street, NW, in 1913.

My mother was a housewife. She was a member of the Mount Carmel Baptist Church and sang in the choir there. She did a lot of needlework and sewing for the family. I can remember a white dress she made for me and embroidered "French dots" on it. Mama read to us a lot. I can remember sitting with her on the front porch reading the comics.

When I joined Mount Carmel Church in 1937, several members, including the pastor's daughters, Mrs. Lottie Adams and Mrs. Gertrude Swancy, said they had known my mother well. Mrs. Ward Brown, Avonia Brown Williams' mother, was from Lynchburg and had been a good friend of my mother. Avonia has been a deaconess and staunch member of Mt. Carmel Baptist Church for many years. Avonia and I were in Sunday school class #4 together for many years.

Sometime around the first of February in 1926 my mother became ill. I was six years old, and my sister, Edna, was eight. My grandparents came from Lynchburg to help take care of the house and family. After about two weeks of illness, my mother died on February 22, 1926, at the age of 33. Her funeral arrangements were handled by the Frazier Funeral Home at the corner of Florida Avenue and Fourth Street, NW, At that time, it was customary to have the body viewed at home before the funeral and a crepe (flower spray) hung on the door of the house. The funeral was held at Mount Carmel Baptist Church, Third and Eye Streets, NW. The burial was at Harmony Cemetery on Rhode Island Avenue, NE near Tenth Street, where the Metro subway station is located now.

The cemetery and body remains were moved to Landover, Maryland, to the Harmony Cemetery's new location.

MY MOTHER'S SISTERS AND BROTHERS

Aunt Nannie

The second oldest child of Sandy and Bettie Garland was Nannie. She was born in 1894. She probably moved from Lynchburg to Washington about 1915. There is a postal card (undated) written to her at 2024 Fourth Street, NW, Washington, D.C. She might have been staying with my parents.

Aunt Nannie married a man named Otis Wallace. I do not know much about him. They bought a home at 431 Third Street, NE, and were living there when I was a little girl. Uncle Otis worked as a Pullman porter on the railroad and traveled a good bit. After he retired, they had a home built in Gordonsville, Virginia, and were living there when Uncle Otis passed away. She later married Delaware Rowe. Aunt Nannie did not have any children.

Nannie Garland Rowe

After Mr. Rowe died, Aunt Nannie sold the house in Gordonsville and had a home built in Lynchburg where her sister Mildred was living. She lived in Lynchburg in her new house for a while then she sold that house and moved back to Washington where she bought a house at Tenth and Emerson Street, NE. It was in the same block where the future Superintendent of Schools, Floretta Dukes McKenzie, lived at that time.

Aunt Nannie was a member of Mount Carmel Baptist Church and used to attend Sunday school there. However, she was not the one who told me to join Mount Carmel. I did not know she was a member there until I saw her there one Sunday when I attended the church at the invitation of my dear friend, Hattie Walton.

Aunt Nannie had one of her brother's (Sandy) wife's relatives, a Miss Woody, living with her on Emerson Street. One day, Miss Woody notified Uncle Sandy that Aunt Nannie had gone shopping then returned home and died suddenly that same day. She died on July 10, 1969, of a heart attack.

Some pictures taken by Charles H. Bruce

Florence Glover Scott and children

Nannie, Florence, and Mildred Garland ca. 1911

Another Charles Bruce photo, shows Aunt Goldie, standing left, next to Marietta's mother Florence Garland. Others pictured are unknown.

It was mentioned earlier in this story that Linda became more interested in the family history after she helped clean up Cousin Connie's house on Manor Place. Among the treasures in the house was a collection of about 250 professional-quality photos of "middle class" African Americans taken between 1908 and 1920, we were led to believe, by Connie's father, Charles H. Bruce, who married Marietta's great aunt Goldie. Duplicates of two of the photos that were in the collection were later found among Marietta's photos. And the ones in Marietta's collection had the stamp Charles H. Bruce on the back and names of some of the people in the pictures! The Charles Bruce photos are now at the Northeastern University (NEU) Archives. We donated them after we learned that NEU was very interested in documenting the history of their neighborhood, including that of the African Americans who once lived there in the "South End" of Boston. One of the pictures was this one of Florence Glover (Scott) and two of her children. was this one of Florence Glover (Scott) and two of her children. It was among Marietta's memorabilia from HER mother Florence Garland Stevens…Apparently Bettie Glover Garland had named her first child Florence after her sister Florence. (See Glover family chart for more information about the relationships.)

Another Charles Bruce photo shows Florence Garland, Mildred Garland, and Nannie Garland. This photo was probably taken in Boston; Mildred and Nannie had likely gone there to visit their sister, Florence, and their grandparents and other relatives who were living in Boston about 1911. We have determined that the Charles Bruce photos were all taken between 1908 and 1920.

The photo collection can be seen online at http://repository.neu.edu/collections/neu:132512/contents/0

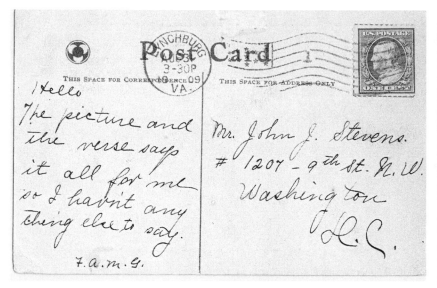

Two more postcards addressed to Florence.

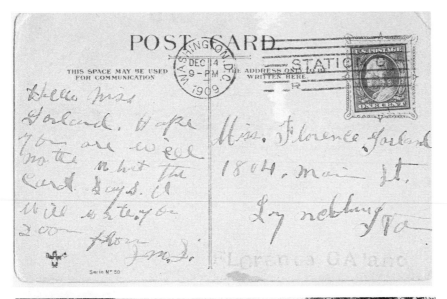

Hello Miss
Garland. Hope
you are well
note what the
card says. It
will be steyou
soon from
J.M.S.

Miss Florence Garland
1804, Main St.
Lynchburg Va.
Florence GA and

Amherst County Road,
Lynchburg, Va.

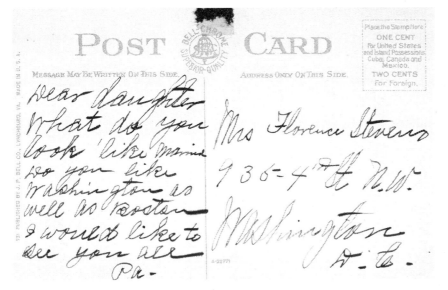

Dear Daughter
What do you
look 'like mama
Do you like
Washington as
well as Boston
I would like to
see you all
Pa.

Mrs Florence Stevens
936-4th St N.W.
Washington
D.C.

Uncle Jack

Uncle Jack in front of the family home on Main Street ca 1918

My mother's oldest brother was John Wesley Garland. We called him Uncle Jack. He was born in Lynchburg, Virginia, on February 22, 1899. I do not know when Uncle Jack came to Washington. He used to visit us occasionally when I was a little girl. He served in the Navy for a while and received an honorable discharge. Uncle Jack never married. In his later years, he lived with a family at the corner of 12th and Rhode Island Avenue, NW, Edna and I visited him there from time to time. As far as I know, he did not have an automobile. Even in his eighties he would walk wherever he wanted to go in this area. Perhaps that exercise helped him stay healthy. He would visit us and come when I invited him for dinner especially at holiday time. For some reason, I do not know why, he did not keep in regular touch with his sisters and brother, and they did not seem to keep in close touch with him. He lived longer than any of the other children of Sandy and Bettie Garland.

Uncle Jack became ill in 1987 and was a patient at Howard University Hospital, at 2041 Georgia Avenue, NW. Edna and I visited him there. I was the last family member to see him alive. He died on July 27, 1987, of liver failure. He was 87 years old. His will stated that he did not want a funeral and he left his body to Howard University for scientific study.

Uncle Sandy

Sandy Asbury Garland Jr.

My mother's brother, Sandy Asbury Garland, Jr., was born October 22, 1901. I do not know what year he came to Washington but he would visit us on Fourth Street from time to time. Sometime in 1926 he married Lillian Woody. They bought a home at 2409 E Street, NE in the Kingman Park area of Washington, DC. They lived at that location for the entirety of their lives. They did not have any children. They were active members of the Kingman Park Association and also The Appomattox Club of Washington.

Aunt Lil, as I called her, told me that the Rev. Sandy A. Garland, Sr., had given them the $350.00 down payment for their house. Sandy, Jr., worked for a while as a redcap at Union Station. Later he worked for thirty-five years at the Justice Department in Washington, D.C. At the time of his retirement, he was serving as a library assistant in the Administrative Division at the Justice Department.

In his later years Uncle Sandy had begun to ail. He was fitted with a heart pacemaker and passed away a short time after that. He died on October 31, 1985, at D.C. General Hospital at the age of 84. His funeral was held at Metropolitan Baptist Church, 1225 R Street, NW, on November 6, 1985, and he was buried at Fort Lincoln Cemetery.

Uncle Sandy's wife, Lillian Woody Garland, worked in the federal government as a cafeteria worker. Some of her family lived in Amherst, Virginia, near Lynchburg. She retired after getting burned at work with a container of hot coffee. Her brother and a sister lived in Washington, D.C. Her sister had one child, Jean Wilson. I met Jean sometime after she married Dr. Lloyd Watts, an obstetrician.

Over the years, I heard Uncle Sandy and Aunt Lil talk very favorably about Jean. Jean was raised by an older cousin, Louise Woody, after her mother died. They lived on 11th Street, NW, near Kenyon Street. Jean taught elementary school in Washington, DC, before her marriage. Jean and Lloyd now live in New York and she corresponds with Edna and me regularly. She is a very lovely person. I wish I had known her years before, but I didn't meet Jean until shortly before Uncle Sandy passed away. Jean died of cancer in 2011.

Aunt Mildred

Rev. and Mrs. Sandy A. Garland, Sr.'s youngest child was Mildred. She was born in Lynchburg, Va. in August 1905. She completed high school there and then came to Washington. She stayed with my parents while she studied at Miner Normal School, then a two-year teachers college school not far from where my parents lived.

After completing her studies at Miner Normal, in about 1922, she returned to Lynchburg. She married Edward H. Brown and they had three children: Edwina, Carolyn, and Edward H. Brown, Jr., (Sonny).

Aunt Mildred was a member of the Eighth Street Baptist Church and played the piano there. She would write to Edna and me after we moved to Pennsylvania. Even though she must have been busy with her own family and activities, she found time to keep in touch with us even though she never visited us there.

Not many people owned automobiles back then, and travel from state to state was limited. Aunt Mildred ailed toward the latter portion of her life. She passed away on October 12, 1971, at the age of 66. She had a heart problem. Her funeral was held at Eighth Street Baptist Church.

Uncle Edward worked as a porter in Lynchburg and had a grocery store next door to their house at 1709 Bedford Avenue, Lynchburg, Virginia, in the Rivermont section of the city. Aunt Mildred helped out in the grocery store and Uncle Edward was always very friendly. I do not know anything about his side of the family. He died December 11, 1986, at well over 90 years of age. (See the news article about Uncle Edward on page 42.)

Mildred Garland Brown

Mildred Garland Brown and children: Carolyn, Edward (Sonny), Edwina in front of 2024 4th Street when visiting Washington, ca 1942

The house that Uncle Edward built at 1709 Bedford Avenue with Brown's Grocery Store next door.

1712 Bedford Ave
Lynchburg, VA
8-28-39

Dear Edna:

Here's hoping you and family are well. We are on the go, altho It rains a lot and keeps every thing all messed up.

I wish you had come down here when you went to D.C. It is only a 5 hr ride from there and fare 5.20 round trip. If you had written and told me you expected to be in D.C. I could have made arrangements to spend a weekend there, I would like to see you again, it's been years since I've seen you.

I am enclosing money for the rent from Main St house for 6 months. Feb. Mar. April amount came to $33.75. Fire insurance to the amount of $9.58 left $24.17 to be divided into fifths as usual which is $4.83 half of that is $2.41 apiece for you children. May, June, July also $33.75. $15.28 had to be taken out for yearly taxes leaving $18.47 to split 5 ways making $3.69 each and half of that Is $1.84 for you and Marietta.

The amount is small but taxes have to be paid yearly as you know and insurance kept in case of careless renters. Then again the fifth that comes to you all has to be split in half, but it's good when it comes as I know every little bit can help.

No, I haven't been anywhere this summer as Mr. Brown didn't get any vacation, he hasn't had one for several years. I need some rest away from home and store as my nerves have been bad since the spell of sickness I had in Feb.

You should be glad that you keep well physically. It means so much. Take care of your health because you certainly lose something when it's gone.

I want to run up to D.C. the weekend of Labor Day in case Sandy comes down here. He said he was.

All send love to you all.

Yours truly,

Aunt Mildred

Linda: Aunt Mildred and Uncle Edward were in charge of the "home house" at 1804 Main Street in Lynchburg that was left by Grandpa Garland—Mildred's father and Marietta's grandfather. This letter was found among Auntie Edna's things (in 2010). Note how Aunt Mildred regularly sent Edna and Marietta their portion of the rent received.

The rent was split between Grandpa Garland's five children—Sandy, Jack, Nannie, Mildred, and Florence. Since Florence was deceased, her share went to Edna and Marietta. It wasn't much but I'm sure they were happy to have it! Tuition at Howard University was only $25 a semester in 1939 and you could buy a pair of shoes for $1.00! Aunt Mildred was very nice to keep this up over the years.

P.S. The tenants in Main St moved out last week. Chum went over and locked up everything Monday. The lady got married and moved to her husband's home.

1715 Bedford Ave.
Lynchburg Va.
8-28-39

Dear Edna:

Here's hoping you and family are well. We are on the go, altho' it rains a lot and keeps every thing all messed up.

I wish you had come down here when you went to D.C. it is only a 5 hr. ride from there & fare 5.20 round-trip. If you had written and told me you expected to be in D.C, I could have made arrangements

---

2

to spend a week-end there. I would like to see you again, it's been years since I've seen you.

I am enclosing money for the rent from Main St. house for 6 months. Feb. Mar. April - amount came to $33.75. Fire insurance to the amount of $9.58 left $24.17 to be divided into fifths as usual. which is $4.83 half of that is $2.41 apiece for you children. May June July also $33.75. $15.28 had to be taken out for yearly taxes. Leaving $18.47 to be split 5 ways making $3.69 each and half of that $1.84 for you & Marietta.

3

The amount is small, but taxes have to be paid yearly as you know, and insurance kept in case of careless renters. Then again the fifth that comes to you all has to be split in half, but it's good when it comes, as I know how every little bit can help.

No, I haven't been anywhere this summer, as Mr. Brown didn't get any vacation, he hasn't had one for several years, I need some rest away from home & store as my nerves have been bad since the spell of sickness

---

4

as I had in Feb.

You should be glad that you keep well physically. It means so much. Take care of your health, because you certainly lose something when it's gone.

I want to run up to D.C. the week-end of Labor Day in case Sandy comes down there. He said he was.

All here send love to you all.

Yours truly,
Aunt Mildred.

P.S. The tennants in Main St moved out last week. Chum went over & locked up every thing Monday. The lady got married & moved to her husband's home.

'Anyone who values life must have inspiration and work to that end. If you don't have it, you must work at getting it before you work at anything else.'

I. Brown

The sugar-coated world has been far from his mind all his life as he strives for more concrete values

Inspiration

'It's not how high you climb ... it's how you continue to climb'

By LAWRENCE HUGHES
Staff Writer

He opens the door to his modest home with a smile of wisdom not borne of age, but of discipline. The sugar-coated world has been far from his mind all his life as he strives for more concrete values.

For example, inspiration.

"Anyone who values life must have inspiration and work to that end. If you don't have it you must work at getting it before you work at anything else. It's not how high you climb that counts, it's how you continue to climb," says Edward H. Brown, warehouseman and philosopher.

It has been said that a person is what he lives. Brown wears a tie and suit coat every day — a fitting symbol of the self-respect he has; he smokes a large cigar befitting his self-worth; and he is open and honest because of self-pride.

He says his long and successful life should be credited to God, honesty and to living a life of discipline. Brown isn't rich by material standards and his lifestyle would be considered strikingly austere by many of worldly insight. Yet, as

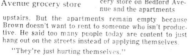

Brown outside his Bedford Avenue grocery store

he approaches his 87th birthday in March, Brown has accomplished goals that take a lifetime, forsaking shorter fleeting fancies for a more permanent happiness.

He sent six children — three of his own and three grandchildren — through college, bought a lot and built a house on it at age 17, invested in a loan cooperative that today occupies a large building in Lynchburg, bought property to rent, and opened a grocery store in 1920.

When he went to Europe during World War I, his friends said he would never be able to make the payments on his house, yet he not only kept the house but saved a substantial sum to buy his store.

Brown qoutes President James Garfield, saying, "If I hope to be anything, I must first make myself a man." Brown followed Garfield's words, working "on being a man first," all his life.

"I always said to God, when I grow up to be a man and

have a family I won't be as poor as (I was as a child). I didn't get an education so I thank God for raising me each level."

He began at the age of 8, making $8 a month as a "jumper" helping deliver milk until he learned the milk route. He said that his deliveries were primarily out in the country, along the now built-up Bedford Avenue and Rivermont Avenue area. After two years of deliveries, he moved up to another dairy that didn't pay higher wages, but did present him with an opportunity that influenced the rest of his life.

"All the wealthy people had nurses that I met as I delivered milk. I told a nurse I was quitting my job and she told her boss, Mrs. Davidson, who told her husband, Mr. Davidson, who said if I wanted a job he'd give me one." Mr. Davidson was an owner of Davidson Brothers Merchandise Brokers, a major merchandiser of produce and canned goods.

"He said he'd give me a job at his warehouse and I was there for 50 years — since 1912 — in the same building," Brown said, adding that over those years the building changed hands three times. It now houses Conners Produce Co.

Brown still owns the grocery store on Bedford Avenue and the apartments upstairs. But the apartments remain empty because Brown doesn't want to rent to someone who isn't productive. He said too many people today are content to just hang out on the streets instead of applying themselves.

"They're just hurting themselves."

In short, "It would take a very special person for me to rent out those rooms," he said. Brown said he is polite to underachievers that he meets day-to-day, but has no patience if they aren't trying.

"Opportunities are looking for the person who is worthwhile finding," he said, adding, "If you can apply what you know, you will have a good life." But too many don't apply it, he said. Not only should a person apply what he knows, but he should "never let anyone else know it better than he."

Brown wears a tie and coat every day — a fitting symbl

Garland cousins
Marietta and Edna with their Garland first cousins Mattie Brown (cousin Edward "Sonny"
Brown's wife), Carolyn Brown, Edna, Edwina Brown Beverley, and Marietta, ca. 1990.

Marietta with aunts and uncles ca. 1965
Front row (l-r): Linda, Martin, Marietta, Aunt Lillian
Back row (l-r): Edna, Uncle Sandy, Aunt Nannie, Uncle Edward, Aunt Mildred
Not Pictured: Uncle Jack

Edwina, Edward (Sonny) Brown, Jr.;Marla, Col. Alfred Elliott, III; Edward (Teddy) Brown, III. Margo and Carolyn Brown looking at family memorabilia while at Auntie Edna's 90th birthday celebration at Eric and Linda's home in 2007. Edwina, Sonny, and Carolyn are the children of Mildred and Edward Brown. They grew up at 1709 Bedford Avenue in Lynchburg. Edwina and Carolyn have been active in preserving Lynchburg African American history.

Paula Kay Beverley Patrom, sister of twins Margo and Marla Beverley, with her husband Daniel, ca. 2014

Twins Marla Beverley Burch
and Margo Beverley Elliott with their mother Edwina Beverley.

CHAPTER 4

Edna Hortense Stevens, My Sister

My parents named their second child Edna Hortense Stevens. She was born at 2024 Fourth Street, NW, on May 22, 1917. Edna attended Lucretia Mott Elementary School which was located at Fourth and Bryant Streets, NW. It was torn down about 1970 and replaced by a new structure called the Katie C. Lewis Elementary School.

I can remember that a man named Walter used to walk with some of the little children up Fourth Street to the school and helped to see that the children arrived at school safely. Walter, as I recall, was a bit "slow" and did not have a job. He lived with his sister, Julia West Hamilton, about a block or two from where we lived. Mrs. Hamilton was a well-known leader in the Colored community at that time. Her name and work are still remembered by the Julia West Hamilton League, a civic association that was named in her honor.

Benetta Bullock, the daughter of Reverend Bullock, pastor at Third Street Baptist Church, was one of Edna's elementary school classmates. Rev. Bullock was very prominent among the church population and in the community. He and his family lived at 408 T Street, NW, about two blocks from our house.

Edna ca. 1937

Rev. Bullock and his wife had eight children. Bennetta was working on her master's degree at Howard when I was an undergraduate student there. She continued her studies and was one of the few Black women to earn a Ph.D. degree during those years. She later became principal of Cardozo High School.

Bennetta married Walter Washington, a Howard student from Georgia. He became prominent as a worker in the District of Columbia government. He was appointed head of the District of Columbia Government's Alley Dwelling Authority and was instrumental in having project houses for the poor built in Southeast Washington.

I think it was a mistake to have so many poor people located together in one area. It probably contributed to the high rate of crimes committed in Southeast to this day.

Walter Washington was later elected the first Black mayor of the District of Columbia. Bennetta died about 1989. Walter remarried and continues to live in the same house at 408 T Street, NW. [Walter Washington died in 2003.]

One of Bennetta's brothers, William, was a year ahead of me at Howard University. He became a physician and set up his office at 408 T Street, NW, where his

Edna ca. 1960

brother George had practiced before he was killed in an automobile accident. William died relatively young of a heart problem. One of Bennetta's sisters was principal of Thomas Elementary School in Washington, D.C.

In August of 1927, my father arranged for his sister, my Aunt Ida, to come to Washington and take us back to Pennsylvania to live with her family. Edna entered the sixth grade at Duquesne Grammar School, moved on through Junior High and on to the Duquesne High School.

Edna was baptized at Jerusalem Baptist Church by Reverend Bryant when she was about twelve years old. She had a nice voice and sang in the junior choir. Edna married Luther H. McIntyre when she was in her teens and moved to live with him at 111 Jewel Street, Duquesne, Pennsylvania. Her husband was well-known in the community and was treasurer of the Jerusalem Baptist Church. He worked in one of the offices at the Carnegie Steel Mill. His hobby was making various kinds of candy that he either sold or gave away.

In 1941, the United States entered World War II. Many people came to Washington from all over the country when the government needed workers to help with the war effort. In Pennsylvania, Edna had taken and passed an examination for a government job. Since there were no good paying jobs available in the Duquesne, Pennsylvania, area, in October of 1942, she arranged with her husband that she would come to Washington to work on a three-month temporary appointment at

Edna & Mother ca. 1923

CONGRATS—Mrs. Marjorie S. Joyner, left, national supervisor of the Mme. C. J. Walker School and guest speaker at the commencement exercises in Washington, D. C., chats with two of the graduates after the commencement at the Walker Memorial Baptist Church in Washington, D. C., Mrs. Edna McIntyre and Mrs. Elizabeth Housley, and at right is Mrs. Louise G. Behlin, manager and instructor of the school.—Cabell Photo.

Edna with Marjorie Stewart Joyner at Madam Walker School Graduation 1957.

Edna with good friends Mary Brown and Mary Bumbry.

the Bureau of Engraving and Printing, located at Fourteenth and C Streets, SW, Washington, DC.

I had also received an appointment to work at the Bureau of Engraving and Printing in December of 1941. Prior to this time, few Colored people were appointed to government jobs except as laborers. Edna made many nice friends there. Among them were Vera Eggleston Perkins, Mary Brown, and Mary Bumbry. Mary Brown and Mary Bumbry were here at my house for a party I gave for Edna when she reached eighty years old in May of 1997. Vera and Mary Brown have died but Mary Bumbry is still one of her closest friends.

Shortly after Edna came to Washington to begin her job at the Bureau, she and I were living at 2024 Fourth Street, NW, with our father when Martin and I decided to marry. Edna was matron of honor at our wedding. Her husband and Aunt Ida came from Pennsylvania for the ceremony. Edna had just planned to work the original three month assignment. However, at the end of the three month period, her appointment at the Bureau (few called the agency by its full name) was extended because many war workers were needed. She then worked "on the press" as a printer's assistant and continued working at the Bureau in other divisions. While working at the Bureau she took lessons in cosmetology at the Madam C. J. Walker College of Beauty Culture and received a certificate on October 25, 1957. She also attended sewing classes at night at the D.C. School's Franklin Building at Thirteenth and K Streets, NW.

Edna and Luther McIntyre were divorced in 1949. Neither of them ever married again. Edna continued to work at the Bureau until her retirement in 1973 after thirty-one years of excellent service for which she received an award. Edna joined

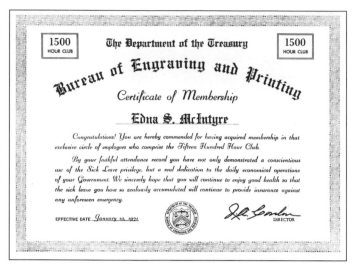

the Mount Carmel Baptist Church about 1945. She rides with me to Sunday school and morning service almost every Sunday. She is a member of the Dan (month of May) Tribe of the Missionary Circle at the Church, and a member of Sunday Church School Class No. 4.

Edna moved to 744 Girard Street, NW, Apartment No. 210 in 1960. Her friend and co-worker, Vera E. Perkins had an apartment at that address, No. 207, right across the hall. Vera worked at the Bureau and later taught elementary school. Vera had earned a Master's degree but teaching jobs were limited so she first took what she could find—the job at the Bureau as a printer's assistant. Many Colored people with college degrees worked as mail carriers and laborers until they could find an opening in their field of study. Office jobs were very limited for Colored people until World War II was well under way.

Below: Old postcard showing the Bureau of Engraving and Printing where Edna worked for over 30 years. Marietta also worked here for a few years before starting her teaching career. This caption is on the back of the postcard: The "Bureau of Printing and Engraving is a branch of the treasury. It employs about 4,000 people and prints the Government Bonds and the National Currency, military, naval and diplomatic commissions, passports, postage and revenue stamps and other Government documents."

The Bureau was one agency that did hire Colored in limited numbers before the War. The work was not professional. It consisted mostly of assisting printers printing currency, war savings bonds, and postage stamps. All of these items after they had been printed had to be counted, stacked, examined for flaws, and prepared for shipping.

Almost all of the supervisors were White although they did not have the education that most of the Colored workers had. I remember one White supervisor who kept a wad of snuff in her jaw. Security there was very tight. Workers had to ask permission to use the restroom and to go out in the hall to make a phone call.

Tours are now conducted at the Bureau of Engraving and Printing. Visitors can look down and view the various procedures carried out there. It looks quite different than when I worked there.

48

Working with currency has from time to time tempted some of the employees to walk out with some of it. I remember reading in the paper about two of the people who worked with the finished currency and thought they could get away with taking some but were caught and sentenced.

As of this writing in 2001, Edna still lives at 744 Girard Street, NW. She has probably lived there longer than any of the other residents. She seems to be getting along quite well physically and gets out and around when she wants to. [*Linda: Auntie moved to Springvale Terrace Assisted Living Facility in December 2010.*]

Linda: Carnegie Steel Mills are where many men—Black and White—were able to get jobs in the early part of the 20th century, including during the depression. The mills were named after Andrew Carnegie, the great industrialist who also gave away millions to build public libraries throughout the United States including libraries at historically Black colleges and universities.

Steel Mills like this were throughout southwestern Pennsylvania until the 1980s when the U.S. began purchasing steel from Japan and China. I remember visiting Pittsburgh/Duquesne with my mother on the occasion of her high school reunion (1965?) and thinking that Pittsburgh was the dirtiest city! There was dust from the mills everywhere! By the 1970s the city had been cleaned up considerably and is now a beautiful city along the three rivers! Mommy used to tell stories of the girls having to wash the dirty bathtub after Uncle Willie and her boy cousins bathed after working in the steel mills all day!

Elizabeth Brumfield pointed out in her book *An Ordinary Man: Black Power in Overalls* that African Americans, like the European immigrants who also worked in the mills, shared the same dream—the chance for equal opportunity.

This badge from Carnegie Illinois Steel Corporation has Winston Stevens' signature underneath the photo and must have belonged to Aunt Ida and John Stevens' brother Winston. It was with Marietta's papers.

49

CHAPTER 5

ELIZABETH JOHNSON LEE
FIRST COUSIN, RAISED AS A SISTER

Linda: Elizabeth "Sis" Lee was one of the cousins with whom Marietta and Edna were raised and remained close throughout the years. I always enjoyed visiting her and playing with her sons—my fun cousins! Her youngest son, Granville and I attended high school together and "hung out" with friends. Mom (also Granville's godmother) would often let Granville drive her car when we went to parties. (dubious decision?)

As stated previously, Marietta and Edna were raised like sisters with their cousins in Duquesne. These cousins were children of my mother's father, John's, sister Ida Stevens Johnson. Elizabeth, who with her husband Clyde later moved to Washington, was always close. In fact, the oft-told story goes that I told my mother that if she ever had to give me away, just give me to Aunt Beth as I called Aunt Elizabeth. I always enjoyed spending the night at their house and Elizabeth and Clyde's youngest son and I were close during our childhood and teenage years. Whenever I asked Mom if I could go to a party, she would ask, "Is Granville going?" as if things would be ok if Granville was going. Oh boy...

Aunt Beth was very active with the Beauty Culturists League and traveled to their conventions most years. Marietta often assisted her with typing and organizing the programs for these events. I remember that later, granddaughter Sabrina assisted her as well. Elizabeth's sister Bertha, a hairdresser in Lynchburg also attended many of these conventions. Aunt Edna, who attended Madame Walker Beauty School but never worked full-time as a hairdresser, attended these sometimes and I remember that when they had local—Washington—events, my mother and I also attended sometimes.

Clyde and Elizabeth Lee ca 1990

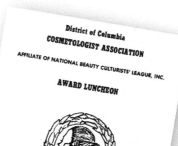

District of Columbia
COSMETOLOGIST ASSOCIATION
AFFILIATE OF NATIONAL BEAUTY CULTURISTS' LEAGUE, INC.

AWARD LUNCHEON

1961   1975

Edna, Bertha Johnson Gilbert, Kenneth Lee, Bernice Lee, Clyde Lee, and little Sabrina Lee, about 1966. Photo taken at our house on Randolph Street.

MRS. ELIZABETH JOHNSON LEE
(WOMAN OF THE YEAR)

Mrs. Elizabeth J. Lee was born in Holden, West Virginia and raised and educated in Duquesne, Pennsylvania. After her marriage to James C. Lee, she moved to Washington, D. C.

Having studied cosmetology at the Friendly Beauty School, she has done further studies under such International artists as Enny of Italy and Otto of Vienna. She holds a Masters Degree from the Institute of the National Beauty Culturist League, inc.

Her civic and religious activities include:

1. Volunteer work as Chairman of Health Survey with the Frederick Douglass Housing Development during which time she requested that a Dental and Well Baby Clinic be set up in that area and organized a committee to make clothes for needy children.

2. She has served as president of Chapter 265 since 1959, which under her leadership was credited with many accomplishments. She continued the program to dress hair for children at Junior Village. Contributed to the Research Center, Bakers Dozen, Heart and Cancer Funds, Baskets for Needy Children at Christmas time, served as Co-Chairman for 1965 National Beauty Culturist Convention, and Trade Show Chairman, Washington, D.C.; 1966 Trade Show Chairman, Oklahoma City. Was honored as "Woman of the Year" at the 1966 convention in Oklahoma by the National Beauty Culturist League, Inc. She has held office as Vice President of District Cosmetologist Association; financial Secretary of Middle Atlantic Region III; Parliamentarian for Delta Chapter, Theta Nu Sigma Sorority and at present is a member of the Trustee Board of the National Beauty Culturist League, Inc.

She is the mother of 4 sons.

Elizabeth and Clyde Lee of Blainesville recall many fond remembrances together

Staff photo by Jeb Caudill

Hard workers

Lees' work ethic pays off in numerous memories

By DOROTHY NOBLE SMITH
Special Correspondent

Elizabeth and Clyde Lee were very young adults during the Great Depression.

They were born and raised in a small southern town where "colored" lived and went to school separately from whites. They knew the lack of a high school education could be a barrier, but they never let that stop them.

"A person has to have some reason to get up and try to help themselves," Elizabeth said as Clyde nodded his approval. "If you sat down every day and said, 'I can't do this or I can't do that,' then you can't. But, if you decide to work, you can find something to do."

Clyde found work hauling coal to the furnace in McKeesport, Pa. This job was particularly hard for Clyde as he was allergic to the water which was available to drink. The water disagreed with his system and one day, while working in the heat, he became so ill he stretched out on a wheelbarrow. Naturally, when he was seen resting, he was fired.

"The Depression was still with us," he said, "and I needed a job."

Fortunately, the firing occurred in the early summer. He moved back to his native Luray and got a job at Skyland, the expensive summer resort in the Blue Ridge Mountains owned by George Freeman Pollock. Clyde's job was waiting on tables. He is the only local person still living who worked for the flamboyant Pollock.

His memories of life at Stony Man bring that place alive.

"There was horseback riding every morning," he said. "We woke up with Pollock playing the old bugle. Music and dancing every night. Sometimes I filled in with the trumpet. You see, Pollock loaned an instrument to anyone who wanted to play. I wasn't much good, but so much was going on they didn't notice."

During these years, Mrs. Lee, a self-taught beautician, was fixing hair and enjoying every minute of it.

"It just came naturally to me," she said.

Her aunt suggested she go to New York City and go to beauty school. She arrived there with no money. However, she managed to get a job working for a family in Brooklyn.

51

The boy always insisted that only I could put him to bed," she said. "This meant a late stay every night."

Mrs. Lee worked there for about 18 months.

"They treated me fine. They gave me all their discarded clothes and this was a real help," she said.

Elizabeth's next job was much better. She got twice the pay and only worked half the time. The sons in the family were all lawyers. The family gave her all their discarded clothes which were fine garments.

"Then I received a letter from my mother," Mrs. Lee said. "She wrote, 'I am as low as low can be.' I arrived home and Ma looked fine. I asked why she wrote that she was as low as could be. She answered, 'I was lying down on the floor when I wrote to you'."

Clyde Lee, looking for work, heard of some in Duquesne, Pa. That's where Elizabeth was then teaching. He went there and the couple has now been married 57 years.

He got a job working at the steel mill in McKeesport. "It was a job," Clyde said.

The couple went to Washington, D.C. upon the insistence of relatives and parents. They lived in public housing in Anacostia, Md. Elizabeth realized that the people there needed guidance so she used her influence with those in her area. They were told, "If you want to get ahead you have to work hard. That's what I told them and that's what I did."

Clyde found work in the summer at Catholic Univeristy, waiting on tables, and he waiting on tables in winter at George Washington University.

Elizabeth took a course at Martha Washington Vocational School at the same time Clyde took up tailoring. Unfortunately, he became too busy to make use of it. When Elizabeth finished her course, she was made an instructor.

There was a great need in Anacostia. Elizabeth and her family did a lot of charity work and at Christmas they made and filled baskets for the needy families. As time went on, the enterprise evolved into a committee called, "The Helping Hand".

"Also, every month we went to Jr. Village by bus and dressed the hair of the children," Mrs. Lee said. "Those children were so very happy to see the bus come."

Through hard work, the careers of both Lees moved up. Clyde told this experience, "In 1941, the best job a colored person could get in Washington was as a messenger. I was making $10.80 a week working in the kitchen at the hospital. At that time, everyone was frozen on his job.

"There was an opening as a messenger at the Justice Department. I went to see the administrative officer, a friend had recommended me. He liked me so he wrote a letter to Mr. Jones at the hospital to free me for this position. At this job, I still got $10.80 per week, but it was a better job.

"I worked in the Antitrust Division until President Roosevelt died. There were eight messengers. Each had their own route to deliver twice in the morning and twice at noon. Everytime something went wrong, they said, 'Lee done it.' I was the newest and supposedly they knew better. I finally got tired of that so went to the administrator and asked that I be put on the longest route and to do it alone. From then on, they knew the mistakes were not done by me.

"I made it my habit to keep busy — the others sat around and waited to be called. I watched everything so then I knew there was an urgent messsage to be delivered. Whenever the head of the Justice Department had something that needed to be done, I helped him. One time it was even moving furniture. The Attorney General also liked me, for I helped in his office.

"When Roosevelt died and Truman took office, they wanted to come up with someone Grade A. Anyone with a government job was asked for their education — all the other fellows had at least a high school education," Lee said.

He never attended high school because there was no high school for blacks in Luray.

"Then they asked me if I would take the job of head messenger for the Attorney General," Lee said. "I said 'no' and was told 'the papers are going through right now'."

He also asked for a raise due to added responsibility and received it.

"I always served the meals when there was some big party for Mr. Truman," Lee said. "In a few years the election came along. I was there and everyone was sure he'd lose, but he won and I was there helping."

Lee said that when John Kennedy was elected President, he and his wife "were the first colored people to be invited to the White House.

"Whenever they had parties, they invited Elizabeth and me," Lee said. "We were invited to parties they held in McLean."

Lee worked 35 years for the Department of Justice. He retired in 1988 and received a party and several plaques of appreciation.

Mrs. Lee took a beauty course at Martha Washington Vocation School and received her degree. Then she taught beauty care in the school.

While Mrs. Lee was affiliated with the school, she collected a group from Martha Washington and Cambridge House and chartered a plane for a trip to Jordan and Jerusalem.

In 1949, she started with the Culture League Inc. in Washington.

"They made me assistant to the president," she said. "I surely was kept busy. Every year, for seven years, I raffled cars as a fundraiser. They were always putting on country conventions, each one was a challenge and each involved a lot of traveling. I received many awards from people in each state."

For Mrs. Lee, however, the work was not all awards. Often, she worked long hours and did double jobs. She was often called to come in when others could not. Often, she had to do two jobs instead of just one.

"If you act fussy and don't cooperate, you don't get very far," Mrs. Lee said. "I am grateful I could be involved."

Mrs. Lee said there were some West Indian girls who worked there.

"They ran the elevator at night and attended school during the day," Mrs. Lee said. "I met them at 6 and did their hair so they were ready for school.

"Then too, there were some nights I didn't get home until 6 p.m. You couldn't leave if you had a customer waiting. Many didn't come until after their dinner, then they came to have their hair done. I couldn't say I was closed. I need their money. Clyde and I were working hard to get away from where we were."

All this was accomplished by a girl who started doing hair at 12 years of age, and a boy who got fired from his first job.

Linda: Many people called the school Martha Washington, but it actually was named Margaret Murray Washington Vocational High School, named after the wife of noted educator Booker T. Washington.

The article says Elizabeth and Clyde lived in Anacostia, MD. Anacostia was part of Washington, DC.

Uncle Clyde, Aunt Beth, Kenny, Clyde, Orlando, and Granville ca. 1954

Lee Extended family: Front: Khalila White, Chanise Lee. First row: Clyde Lee, Sr., Elizabeth Lee, Marie Adams, Robert Thompson (Nancy's parents), Eura Jenkins, Marietta Crichlow. Second row: Linda White, Kwame White, Carol Lee holding daughter Krystal lee, Back row: James C. Lee, III (Jamie), James C. Lee, Jr. (Clyde), Kenneth Lee, Granville C. Lee, Jr., Granville Lee, Michelle Lee, Shellie Lee, William (Billy) Lee, Nancy Lee, Orlando Lee, Anthony Lee, ca. 1993.

CHAPTER 6

MARIETTA LOUISE STEVENS CRICHLOW

**Marietta Stevens Crichlow
ca. 1966**

*Linda: Mott Elementary
School, an elementary school
for Colored children was
named for Lucretia Mott, a
noted White abolitionist.*

On the next few pages, I will give a brief sketch of my own background. According to my birth certificate, I was born at 7:30 p.m. on August 20, 1919, at home at 2024 Fourth Street, NW.

Back there then, most women did not go to the hospital to have their babies. I was given the name Mary Etta Louise Stevens, and was named after my father's great aunt, Mary Etta Kinney. Somewhere along the line someone spelled my name Marietta, and that is the way I have spelled it ever since I have been able to read and write.

Some of my playmates in the neighborhood were Almarian Stoakley who lived with her grandparents, Mr. and Mrs. Anderson, across the street at 2017 4th Street NW; Lillian McDaniel who lived at 2032 Fourth Street, NW, and Vivienne Scarborough who lived on Elm Street, around the corner from us. Vivienne is still one of my friends. Almarian, who before her marriage had been a member of Mount Carmel Baptist Church, passed away about five years ago.

Mrs. Anderson, Almarian's grandmother, was from Lynchburg, Virginia, and I think my father might have lived with her when he first came to Washington. Almarian married a Mr. Jackson. She had two lovely children, Velma and Vashon. Lillian's family moved and I have lost track of her.

I attended Lucretia Mott Elementary School at Fourth and Bryant Streets, NW. The building has been torn down and replaced by the Katie C. Lewis Elementary School. My parents entered me in kindergarten in 1923 when I was four years old. After my mother died in February of 1926, my father tried to find someone suitable to take care of us. When I had finished third grade at Mott Elementary School, my father sent my sister and me to Pennsylvania to live with his sister, Aunt Ida L. Johnson, and her family.

When I was at Mott School I can remember I was always at the end of the line for everything. When paper and supplies were passed out, I was the last one to receive them. Sometimes, the teacher would pass out goodies, like candy or peanuts. I can remember one time the teacher passed out Baby Ruth candy bars. The supply ran out just before it got to me. When I grew up and was in charge of a classroom I always tried to be sure that the last person on the list received whatever was passed out. It took me a while to find out why I was always last or left out. The pupils were listed alphabetically and my last name started with an "S."

A MAJOR TRANSITION, MOVING TO PENNSYLVANIA

There are events that take place that leave an indelible impression on a person's life. One of these events happened on February 22, 1926, when my mother, Florence Garland Stevens died.

My father's sister Marie had come from Hot Springs, Virginia, to help and she stayed for about six weeks. I remember my father asking her if she could stay longer. She said, "No, John, I have to return to Hot Springs." She had been employed at the Homestead, a resort at Hot Springs, Virginia, since she was about seventeen years old.

My father was able to get a friend and her husband, Mr. and Mrs. Henry, to come and stay with us. We called her "Mama Henry." She was a very nice lady but after several months, Mrs. Henry had to go into the hospital for surgery and she her husband were no longer able to stay with us.

A Mr. and Mrs. Boyd came and stayed for a while. After they left, no one else came on a permanent basis. After school, Edna and I would stop by a neighbor's house (at Mr. and Mrs. Heathman's home at 2028 4th St.) and wait until Daddy came home from work.

I don't remember ever having a meal served to us by any of the neighbors. With the exception of Mrs. Henry, I do not remember that any of the members at Mount Carmel, where my mother had been member, came to assist.

One of my mother's friends, Josephine Bailey, would invite us over to her house once in a long while, to play with her daughter, Phyllis. Aunt Nannie, my mother's sister, took us to her house a few times on Saturdays, when her husband, who worked as a porter with the railway, was out of town. I do not remember my mother's brothers ever being of any help to us back there then.

In August of 1927, a few days before my eighth birthday, my father's sister, Ida L. Stevens Johnson, came from Elizabeth, Pennsylvania, and took my sister, Edna, and me to live with her and her family.

Uncle Willie (right) in the pulpit

Her husband, Rev. William Preston Johnson, had been visiting his family in Schuyler, Virginia, and he came by our house just before we left for Pennsylvania. He was a nice man. He must have been, to agree to let two young kids join his household when they already had five of their own children and Aunt Ida's brother, Winston, and her niece, Lillian.

When Uncle Willie stopped by Washington, he showed me an interesting cane he carried, although he did not need it for support. It had a carved head on it. I do not remember having seen Aunt Ida prior to this time, although she said she had seen me once. I must have been too young to remember the occasion. We traveled to Elizabeth, Pennsylvania, on the train. My father stayed in Washington and worked.

55

Elizabeth, Pennsylvania, was a coal mining town. My first impression was of Uncle Willie's garden. In our part of Washington, people, as far as I know, did not grow gardens. He grew tomatoes, sweet potatoes, onions, and a lot of other vegetables.

Another interesting thing was the house. It had no running water, gas, or electricity. That took some getting used to for me. In Washington, at the time of my mother's illness, my parents were in the process of having electricity installed in the house. And it had running water. Prior to having electricity installed, the house had gas light. Gas lamps were fastened to the walls. And the streets had gas lights. A man would come along in the evening with a light at the end of a long pole and light the street gas lights. At the house in Elizabeth there was a pump out back. I would try to pump it, but I was almost too light-weight to pull the handle up and down.

At Aunt Ida and Uncle Willie's house we met the rest of their family, and then some. They had five children of their own. George, the eldest, was in his late teens. Emmet was about 15; Elizabeth (Sis) was 13; Albert was about 12, and Bertha was 9. Lillian Garland, Aunt Ida's late sister Mamie's thirteen year old daughter, also was there. And Winston, Aunt Ida's younger brother, lived with them. Edna and I increased the number living in the household to eleven people. When I think back on it, that was quite an effort on the part of Aunt Ida and Uncle Willie.

Several weeks after Edna and I moved to Pennsylvania, the family moved to Duquesne, Pennsylvania, a steel mill town, 13 miles southwest of Pittsburgh. The town of Duquesne received its name from General Duquesne, a Frenchman who fought in the French and Indian War that took place in the area around Pittsburgh. Duquesne was probably about ten miles from Elizabeth. This was a more modern house with electricity, gas, and running water.

I was enrolled in the fourth grade at the Duquesne Grammar School. All of the teachers were White. In Washington, all of our teachers in the segregated school system called Division Two, were Colored. Before I left Washington, I had not given the color of the teachers a thought.

In Duquesne, the authorities probably decided that there were not enough Colored people to set up a separate school for them. Many of our neighbors and most of our classmates were people from eastern Europe—Polish, Hungarian, etc. Lots of people called the Colored people Niggers and the Hungarians, Honkies.

GROWING UP IN THE CHURCH

Jerusalem Baptist Church

The family joined the Jerusalem Baptist Church in Duquesne. It was located at Fifth Street and Grant Avenue. I participated in many programs there. We attended most of the services. Sundays were spent at Sunday school, morning service, evening Baptist Young People's Union (BYPU) and evening service. Our friends were there too and it was usually enjoyable. I was baptized by Reverend Bryant in 1929 when I was ten years old.

At the BYPU, an elderly man named Mr. McLemore would hold Bible drills where we would stand at the front of the church and he would call off names of books and chapters of the Bible. The one who found it first would receive a little prize. He would also ask other biblical information. I have a Bible dated April 2, 1936, that I won in a BYPU contest; it was people at the church like Mr. McLemore who encouraged young people to use their minds and try to uplift themselves.

Deacon and Mrs. Hines, the parents of the noted musician, Earl Hines, were members of Jerusalem Baptist Church. Mrs. Hines would come to my Aunt Ida's house and work on the financial reports for the Missionary Society. Nancy Hines, Earl's sister was also a member. She played the piano beautifully. Earl's brother, "Boots" did not attend church services regularly. He liked to shoot pool.

Once Earl Hines visited Jerusalem and the pastor, Rev. George W. White, invited him to come to the front of the church and speak. Jazz was not too acceptable with ministers then. Rev. White told Earl that he hoped that some day he would turn his life around and give up the devil's work. The mother of the famous vocalist, "Sonny Boy" Woods, was a member of Jerusalem. He sang with Louis Armstrong's band. One day he came by Aunt Ida's house and she asked him to sing a song for us. He sang "If I Didn't Care," a very pretty jazz number.

Jerusalem had a number of enlightened, educated people. The church was a member of the Allegheny General Baptist Association and was up to date with its methods. The leaders of the choirs were well trained musicians. Aunt Ida and the girls at 113 Linden Avenue, where we lived, were members of one or another of the choirs. We sang anthems and very pretty church hymns.

When we first joined Jerusalem, I remember that the church did not have enough hymn books to supply all of the members so the leader of the devotions would "outline" the hymn. That is, he would read a couple lines of the hymn and the congregation would sing them. Then, he would read a couple more lines. The Lord will make a way!

Our social life centered around the church. Every year we looked forward to the church picnic that was held at Olympia Park near Duquesne. Everybody would be busy preparing food and getting ready for this big event.

We walked to school and to church. There was a railroad crossing that often had to be crossed before getting to the school. If a train was coming, we often would run and try to get across the tracks to keep us from being late for school. If the train stopped at the station, blocking the crossing, some of the boys would hop the train and go through the openings between coaches.

These were the Depression years and many people were out of work. Some of the young boys would hop the freight train when it stopped and climb to the top of the freight train carrying coal and throw off coal to pick up and take back home so the family could have fuel for their stoves and furnaces. One of the neighborhood youngsters was throwing coal when the train started up. He lost his balance, was tossed to the ground, and the train ran over his legs. Following that, his legs

The Louis Armstrong Band was very popular from the 1920s until Armstrong died in 1971.

Earl "Fatha" Hines, native of Duquesne and noted jazz pianist during World War II. The poster is typical of the times.

Duquesne High School

were shortened above the knee and he would get around by sitting on a scooter with rollers on it. He always seemed to have a smile.

As time went on, I passed to the Duquesne Junior High School and then to Duquesne High School. In the town, there was only one school for each level and the schools were not named for individuals as they are in Washington such as Wilson High School in honor of former President Woodrow Wilson and Dunbar High School in honor of the poet Paul Lawrence Dunbar.

The students at Duquesne High School were required to be a member of one of the two drama clubs—the Adelphians or the Philomethians. I was a member of

LATIN CLUB
Marietta was in the academic track so was required to take Latin in high school.
She also was a part of the Latin club. Marietta is 3rd from left on the front row.

School Savings
THREE YEAR CERTIFICATE

This is to Certify that _Marietta Stevens_

has made a deposit in School Savings every Savings Day for three Years and has not made any withdrawals.

Duquesne
School District

Senior High School
School

J. C. Gillespie
Principal

Anna M. Byers
Teacher

June 7, 1937.
Date

_1936-1937._
Term

Issued in Behalf of the School Savings Depository
BY STANDARD SAVINGS SERVICE, INC., PITTSBURGH, PA.
A pupil earning six certificates in six consecutive years will receive a six year certificate.

School Savings Banking
CERTIFICATE

This is to Certify that _Marietta Stevens_

has made a deposit in School Savings Banking every Bank Day this school year and has not made any withdrawals.

Duquesne
School District

Junior High
School

Fred Haines
Principal

1

W. E. Barber
Teacher

June 1, 1934.
Date

_1933-34_
Term

Issued by Standard Savings Service, Inc., Pittsburgh, Pa.
A pupil earning three certificates in three consecutive years will receive a three year certificate.
A pupil earning six certificates in six consecutive years will receive a six year certificate.

**Savings certificates encouraged young people to manage their money.
They need such programs for children today!**

---

the Adelphians Club. The clubs put on programs in the auditorium alternately every few weeks. I remember reciting a long monologue that I had memorized.

Some of us Colored pupils put on a play at one of these programs that I thought was very nice. The school permitted Miss Ruth Kidd, a member of our church, to direct the play. I was also a member of the Latin Club. If we were headed for an academic career, we had to take Latin—from eighth grade through the twelfth grade. There were other clubs at the school, such as the opera club, that Colored students were not encouraged to join.

While I was in high school, the church selected me to represent the Junior Department of the Sunday School at the Allegheny General Baptist Association Convention in Donora, Pennsylvania. That was a big thing for me. I borrowed my cousin Elizabeth's suitcase. When I reached Donora, I could not find the key to open the suitcase and had to break it open! That was regrettable but I did enjoy the convention. It was my first time spending a few days away without any family members along.

At the end of each school year the schools arranged for a picnic at Kennywood Amusement Park. It was about two miles from Duquesne. Families would prepare picnic baskets and kids would look forward to enjoying the rides and other amusements. There was a dance pavilion that the Colored were not allowed to enter. Yet, at school, we had to repeat the Pledge of Allegiance…"with liberty and justice for all."

In June 1937 I graduated from Duquesne High School. Daddy came from Washington to attend the graduation exercises. The senior prom, that both Whites and Colored attended, was held in the school gymnasium. There were no after-prom activities or out-of-town trips like young people have now and that was good. I think that youngsters do not need too much of that sort of thing. Some now go out on wild parties, get drunk, have automobile accidents and end up in loads of trouble.

None of the high school personnel talked with me about attending college. There were no school counselors in those days. Two adults lived next door to us, Vernon and his brother, Frank Worrell. Frank had attended Howard University as a pre-medical student but dropped out for lack of funds. He was a very professional looking fellow. It was Frank who suggested that I apply for admission to Howard University. He told me where to write and how to go about it. He told me that since my father lived in Washington, it might be fairly convenient for me to return to Washington and attend college there.

In 1967, my husband, Martin, and daughter, Linda, went to Pennsylvania to attend my 30th high school class reunion. There had been fourteen Colored in my graduating class. About six of them were at the reunion. Each graduate had listed in the program bulletin information about his or her accomplishments. It seemed that most of the White girls were housewives all through the years. Only a few had attended college. Of my Colored classmates, four of us attended college. Attending college was not particularly the way to go for young women back then. Women were expected to marry and take care of their husbands and children at home.

During the summer after I graduated from high school, I worked as a clerk in Mr. Walker's grocery store. Mr. Walker was a member of Jerusalem, and his store was about a block and a half away from home. I earned a great big five dollars a week. I was glad to get it. Then, even adult women were paid about five dollars a week when they worked as domestics all day long for White families. Five dollars meant a lot. A loaf of bread could be purchased for five cents. Inflation had not yet set in and the economic Depression was widespread. Now, the youngsters charge at least ten dollars for a few minutes of work cleaning the snow from the front of my house.

60

EAST BORO GLIMPSES

Happenings In the Shadows of the Steel Mills

By ROBERT HUGHEY

Note: A weekly column dedicated to the interest of the people of the East Boro and vicinity. Address all communications to Braddock avenue, Braddock, Pa.

Clippings from the Pittsburg Courier, noted African American newspaper.

The clipping from December 9, 1939, describes cousins Emmet and Ann Johnson's wedding reception at the home of Edna and Luther McIntyre at 111 Jewel Street in Duquesne. The same clipping mentions Edna and Luther's wedding anniversary.

The clipping from July 1935 reports about Marietta's visit to Donora, Pennsylvania, as well as Elizabeth's return to Duquesne.

December 9, 1939
pg. 15

Hear that Mr. and Mrs. Luther H. McIntyre, of 111 Jewel street, Duquesne, observed their sixth wedding anniversary last Thursday.

* * *

E. M. JOHNSONS FETED

Topping off the social while in Duquesne last Thursday evening was the belated reception given in honor of Mr. and Mrs. E. M. Johnson, newlyweds of one month, at 113 Linden street, Duquesne. Upward to 75 guests joined in the merry-making here where highlights consisted of dancing, card playing, parlor games and refreshments. Many and assorted gifts graced the occasion. Attending the affair were: Out-of-towners, Mrs. T. Lynch and Mrs. Mackey of Monongahela, Mr. and Mrs. Thomas Page, Mrs. Hanks, Mrs. Emmett Stevens, Martha Goins and Mrs. Mary Tucker of Pittsburgh; Cleo Barnett and Pearl Martin of Mt. Lebanon, Russell McAbee and James Holloway of Braddock and Claudine Page of Pittsbugh. Among the locals were Mrs. Grace Dickens, Mrs. Woods, Mr. and Mrs. James A. Watson, Mr. and Mrs. John L. Edwards, Mr. and Mrs. W. L. Jordon, Paul Cole, Mr. and Mrs. Robinson, Beatrice Ginyard, Robert Brown, Alrada Queen, L. H. McIntyre, Ruby Robinson, Bertha Johnson, the honored guests and others.

* * *

TALK O' TOWN

Crisp, Breezy Comment on This and that and Those in Smoke Town

The Pittsburgh Courier (1911-1950); Jul 6, 1935; pg. 9

Marietta Stevens of Duquesne represented the Jerusalem Baptist B. Y. P. U. at the convention which convened at the First Baptist Church, Donora. While there she resided with Helen and Alene Blaine.

* * *

Due to the illness of her brother, Elizabeth Johnson of Brooklyn, N. Y., has returned to her former residence in Duquesne.

* * *

See Appendix for more information about Black newspapers.

Linda: Even in Duquesne, folks were trying to work out the issues of "race relations." Some distinguished speakers were listed on the program. It would be interesting to know exactly what the speakers' messages were that day. Interesting that the Negro National Anthem was part of the program. During the 50s and 60s when I was growing up, I don't remember ever hearing or singing it. It wasn't until the late 60s and the re-surgence of Black Power that I began to hear it. Was it that I just missed it or was it that there was a period of time when it was lost??

Growing up in Mt. Carmel, I DO remember Negro History Week and Brotherhood Sun-day. Negro History Week was begun in 1925 by historian Carter G. Woodson and evolved into Black History Month in the 1960s. Perhaps Race Relations Day (like at Jerusalem Church) evolved into Brotherhood Week. They all took place during the 2nd week in February—to coincide with the birthdays of Abraham Lincoln (February 12) and Frederick Douglass (adopted as February 14).

THE PHYLLIS WHEATLEY LITERARY SOCIETY

Presents Their

Third Annual

Race Relation Program

At The

Jerusalem Baptist Church

Duquesne, Pa.

SUNDAY, FEBRUARY 14, 1937

7:30 o'clock

Miss Lillian Walker
Chairman

Program

Song by Congregation	Negro National Anthem
Prayer	
Race Relation Message	
Phyllis Wheatley	Mrs. Hazel Scott
	Rev. J. O. Edwards
	Pastor of Payne Chapel A. M. E. Church
Vocal Solo	Miss Bertha Johnson
You Must Choose	
	Dr. F. B. McClelland
	Professor at Duquesne University
The Value of a Definite Purpose	
Vocal Solo	Mrs. Hazel White
	Miss Peggy Fowler
White and Balck	
	Mrs. W. E. Hill
	Industrial Secretary of the Urban League
Remarks	
Benediction	Announcements

Motto
"Honor Above All"

Color
Green and Silver

Flower
Tea Rose

Personnel

Mrs. Sarah Coles	Miss Louise Jordan
Miss Lillian Walker	Mrs. Edna McIntyre
Miss Maybel Claggett	Miss Bertha Johnson
Mrs. Mildred Jones	Miss Dilcie Rome
Miss Avrilla Rome	Mrs. Willogene Durrah
Miss Gussie Taylor	Miss Marietta Stevens
Miss Moda Godbolt	Miss Sannie Walker

Mrs. Hazel Scott - President

Mrs. Frances Keith Randall - Advisor

NEGRO NATIONAL ANTHEM

Lift every voice and sing,
Till earth and heaven ring,
Ring with the harmonies of Liberty;
Let our rejoicing rise
High as the listening skies,
Let it resound loud as the rolling sea.
Sing a song full of the faith that the dark past has taught us
Sing a song full of the hope that the pres-ent has brought us;
Facing the rising sun of our new day begun,
Let us march on till victory is won.

Stony the road we trod,
Bitter the chast'ning rod,
Felt in the days when hope unborn had died;
Yet with a steady beat,
Have not our weary feet
Come to the place for which our fathers sighed?
We have come over a way that with tears has been watered
We have come, treading our path thro' the blood of the slaughtered,
Out from the gloomy past,
Till now we stand at last
Where the white gleam of our bright star is cast.

God of our weary years,
God of our silent tears,
Thou who hast brought us thus far on the way;
Thou who hast by Thy might,
Led us into the light,
Keep us forever in the path, we pray
Lest our feet stray from the places, our God, where we met Thee,
Lest our hearts, drunk with the wine of the world, we forget Thee;
Shadowed beneath Thy hand,
May we forever stand,
True to our God, True to our Native land.

MEMBERS

Mildred Jones	Edna McIntyre
Lillian Walker	Sannie Walker
Avrilla Rome	Delcie Rome
Willogene Durrah	Louise Jeffries
Mabel Turner	Moda Mae Powell
Marietta Stevens	Bertha Johnson
Hazel Scott	Sarah Coles

Frances Kieth Randall - Club Advisor

---

* * *

Phyllis

Wheatley

Literary

Society

* * *

BACK TO WASHINGTON
AND TO HOWARD UNIVERSITY

In August of 1937 when I was 17 years old, I returned to Washington, DC, to live and to attend Howard University. My father, who lived at 2024 Fourth Street, NW, arranged for me to stay at Mr. Watt's house, 1955 Fourth Street, NW, diagonally across the street from 2024, until June of 1938. I remembered Mr. Watts because he and his wife had a tailor shop at the corner of Fourth & Elm Streets. His wife had passed away and his niece, Emily Diggs, her daughter, Alease, and Alease's husband, Reginald Bridgeford, lived there. I slept on a daybed in the living room and stored my clothes in a suitcase behind the sofa. Mrs. Diggs prepared the meals. Alease was a nice young lady, two or three years older than I. She died in the spring of 1938. I do not know what her physical problem was. She had been ill for several weeks.

Howard University

By June of 1938, the family who had rented all but one room at 2024 had moved out. I went to the Goodwill Store that was then located near the corner of Georgia Avenue and Florida Avenue, NW, and bought furnishings for the house. A married couple named Wilber and Elizabeth Jenkins rented the upstairs front bedroom. His mother lived in the apartment next door above the tailor shop. After Elizabeth and Wilber moved out, Ella and Charles Johnson, a cousin of B. Dennis Rand who worked at the tailor shop, moved in. Ella was a few years older than I. They were a nice couple. Ella and Charles moved out in 1942 but Ella and I remained friends through the years. Ella remarried and was a deaconess at Hemingway Baptist Church at Fifth and P Streets, NW. Her husband, John Cox, was a deacon there. She died in 1997. I attended her funeral.

Marietta and Lillian Stanback were good friends. Here they are pictured about 1940 on Howard University's campus. Lillian married Marietta's cousin Albert. Lillian died in childbirth with Barbara in 1943.

The days and months following my move from 1955 Fourth to 2024 Fourth Street, NW, were very busy ones. I was adjusting to my studies at Howard and keeping house for Daddy. Some of the girls I met at Howard would sometimes come down from the campus and spend Saturday or Sunday night with me. Ann Young, from Malden, Massachusetts, and Jane Diggs from New Jersey were two of them. I have a desk in one of my bedrooms now that Ann gave me after she left Howard. She had bought it for her dormitory room. During the summer, Ann worked for a White family on Dumbarton Avenue, NW. One summer when she went back to Massachusetts, I worked for them for one dollar a day and car fare. Ann married a serviceman on the same day that I got married, November 29, 1942.

When I enrolled as a freshman at Howard, my childhood playmate, Almarian Stoakley who lived across the street from me, also enrolled. A day or two after the beginning of the school year in 1937 Almarian introduced me to a friend of hers named Hattie Walton who, along with Almarian, attended Mount Carmel Baptist Church. This was the beginning of a long, close friendship that lasted until Hattie passed away on July 10, 2001.

JOINING MT. CARMEL BAPTIST CHURCH

It was Hattie who invited me to go with her and her family one Sunday to Mount Carmel, located at 901 Third Street, NW. This was really very strange. There are dozens of Colored churches in Washington, DC, but she invited me to Mount Carmel. When we arrived at the church she introduced me to some of the people who told me that my mother had been a member at Mount Carmel. Reverend W. H. Jernagin was the pastor in 1937. His daughter, Mrs. Lottie Adams, told me she had been a friend of my mother's. There were others, Mrs. Craig and Mrs. Brown, who were also my mother's friends. When I went to Sunday school at Mt. Carmel one Sunday I looked over at the members of Class No. 3 and there was Mrs. Cordelia Henry who took care of us for a while after my mother had died. Mama used to send my sister, Edna, and me to Florida Avenue Baptist Church at 623 Florida Avenue, NW. A young girl who lived nearby used to take us. I thought Mama was a member of Florida Avenue Church. All I can say is maybe it was meant for me to be a member of Mount Carmel.

I joined Mt. Carmel as a member in 1937. I sang in the Junior Choir and was active for a while in the BYPU now called Christian Training Program (CTP). I have taught in the Sunday school there all through the years, first in the children's department. For more than forty years I have been assistant teacher of Adult Class No. 6, a group of lovely ladies, most of them retired now. I have been a member of Class No. 4, formerly called the Teacher's Training Class, ever since I joined the church, and secretary of Class No. 4 for more than 20 years. In 1997, I was appointed to serve as secretary of the Reverend Arthur H. Pace Church Library.

My new friend, Hattie, lived at 1715 Fourth Street, NW, with her mother, Mrs. Louise Meachum, her step-father, Mr. Meachum, and her half-sister, Frances. While walking to her classes at Howard, Hattie would frequently stop by my house and we would walk together up the hill to Howard. (Howard's Alma Mater song states that it is *"Reared against the eastern sky, proudly there on hilltop high..."*) Some days after class, I would walk down to her house with her. Hattie introduced me to many new friends: among them were Gertrude Payne, Avonia Williams, and Martha Archer. One day Hattie said that a few of her friends who lived near her were coming to her house that afternoon. She asked me to come down to her house and meet them. One of the young people that I met that day was Martin Crichlow. I had never heard of such an odd last name. And I thought Martin was the silliest person ever, always saying something funny and cracking jokes. I also met his friend Eugene 'Bud" Ford. Martin and Bud had been classmates at Hampton Institute (now Hampton University).

In June of 1941 I graduated from Howard University with a bachelor of arts degree in sociology. During some of the summers while I had been a student at Howard I worked for the NYA (National Youth Administration). Mrs. Mayes, wife of Dr. Benjamin Mayes, Dean of the School of Religion, was in charge of the District of Columbia's Colored branch of the National Youth Administration. That was a program started by President Franklin Delano Roosevelt to give some

Members of the Coordinating Committee for the Enforcement of the District of Columbia Anti-Discrimination Laws. ca. 1950, picketing to end discrimination in restaurants.
The person holding the "End Discrimination" poster is Mt. Carmel's noted pastor Rev. W. H. Jernagin. To his left is Mrs. Mary Church Terrell, noted community leader. To her left is Rev. R. L. Patterson who was Rev. Jernagan's assistant and who became full pastor in 1958 after Rev. Jernagin died. Rev. Patterson baptized Linda in 1959 at Mt. Carmel. Second from the left in the photo is Reverend Leamon White of Mt. Bethel Church and third from the right is Reverend R.L. Harrison, pastor of Shiloh Baptist Church.

Almarian Stoakley pictured here with her grandmother Alice Anderson lived at 2017 4th Street, NW, across the street from Marietta and also attended Mt. Carmel. Photo of Almarian provided by her daughter Alecia Velma Jackson in 2013. Alecia and Linda had attended Sunday School together at Mt. Carmel and reconnected in 2012 after bumping into each other at a community event.

kind of basic employment to young people. I was interviewed by Mrs. Mayes and received an NYA job.

I worked part-time as a clerk at the Wilson Elementary School at Seventeenth and Euclid Streets, NW, in the testing department under Dr. Howard Long. Mr. Bowie was my supervisor. My job was to help correct and evaluate the intelligence tests that were given to DC public school children. Electric calculators had just become popular. The one I used there was larger than a typewriter. Now, there are calculators that do all sorts of mathematical procedures and are small enough to put in a pocket. One of my co-workers and good friends was Luella Wedlock, who later became professor of political science at Howard University.

During my senior year at Howard, I applied to enter the school of social work and was accepted to study there as a graduate student. That was the field in which there seemed to be a need for workers. However, because of a shortage of tuition funds, when the fall arrived, I continued to work with the NYA.

In 1939, World War II had broken out in Europe and the U.S. and its allies, England and France were fighting against the enemy nations of Japan, Germany, and Italy. On December 7, 1941, the Japanese bombed the United States Naval Base at Pearl Harbor, Hawaii. On December 8, the United States declared war on Japan and a few days later declared war on Germany and Italy. This was to change a lot of things—some for the better and some for the worse. Many young men were

SAVINGS STAMP FOLDER
for holding Stamp Receipts issued through
AUTOMATIC RECEIVING TELLERS
Operated By

INDUSTRIAL SAVINGS BANK

11th and U Streets, Northwest
WASHINGTON, D. C.
FOR THE PROMOTION OF THRIFT

To encourage people to earn and save money
is of vital importance to the individual
and to the nation.

WE WELCOME YOU AT THIS BANK

INTEREST AND SAFETY FOR YOUR SAVINGS

THIS FOLDER IS THE PROPERTY OF

Black banks like Industrial encouraged thrift. This is a copy of Marietta's savings stamp book from 1926. Industrial Bank still serves the community today.

drafted to serve in the war, leaving their jobs to be filled by others. Also, there was a demand for war materials. Lots of jobs opened up to aid the war effort. People came to Washington from all parts of the country to work.

I had applied for a government job and on December 12, 1941, received an appointment to work as printer's assistant at the Bureau of Engraving and Printing, a branch of the United States Treasury Department that was located at Fourteenth and C Streets, NW. My duties were to help place unfinished paper on the printing press that would be printed into currency or savings bonds. I was also assigned to other sections of the Bureau doing such jobs as examining the large sheets of paper money before it was cut into bills, examining bonds, and working at a collating machine that fastened the completed bond to other pulp. For a long time, I worked twelve hours a day, seven days a week.

Before World War II, most government jobs were open only for White people. There were few if any Colored typists or office workers, just laborers who cleaned. The war was a horror, yet it did make better jobs available for Colored people and helped break down the color barrier somewhat.

Washington was a very segregated city in 1941. Colored people were not allowed to sit at lunch counters and eat but they could scrub the floors there. They could not sit beside White people on trains, yet they could work in the White folks' homes cooking their food, taking care of their children. Street cars were driven by Whites. Sales people in the stores were White. Banks and private businesses hired only White clerks. Colored people could not receive care at White hospitals like Georgetown and George Washington. Colored students could not attend certain colleges. (See picture of Mt. Carmel's Rev. Jernagin picketing to end segregation practices in restaurants.)

Yet Colored people survived. They had the Colored Freedmen's Hospital, the Colored banks like Industrial, Colored churches, Colored schools Division Two, and their own social life. U Street, NW, was famous for social life among Colored people. The Lincoln and Republic theaters were very nice. There were social clubs for entertainment like Club Bali where dignified people attended. There are some White churches that have accepted Black members and the National City Christian Church where former President Johnson attended, recently appointed a Black minister, Reverend Jackson as its pastor. So, in a way, things have changed but racism is still subtly around.

In April of 1943, I was transferred to the Procurement Division of the General Services Administration that housed a branch of the Treasury Department. It was located at Seventh and D Streets, SW. I worked for a few years as a clerk typist for one of the purchasing officers. Her name was Ms. Margaret Wager. She was a nice lady. The purchasing officers were responsible for buying supplies for the government that were to be sent overseas to help the allies of the United States in the war. That program was called United Nations Rehabilitation and Relief Association (UNRRA). I typed contracts that were to be sent to companies furnishing the needed supplies. Ms. Wager was responsible for purchasing chemical and medical supplies. I wish that I had known then about investing. I recently read an article about a lady who in the 1940s invested five thousand dollars in two of the chemical companies. In 1997 her stock investment had grown to twenty-two million dollars. Most Colored folks were not then, and many of us are not now, familiar with investing. The Black churches are beginning to encourage their members to join investment clubs.

While I was working in Procurement, I was one of the typists selected to determine the practicability of a new typewriter key arrangement—the Dvorak method. The inventor said that it would work faster since the most used keys were properly placed on the keyboard. It was not widely accepted. I understand that the method is used by some companies these days.

During the years that I worked in Procurement, I also attended night classes at the Cortez Peters Business School located at Ninth and U Streets, NW. When the Cortez Peters School opened, it was said to be a pivotal moment in history. Not only was it the first Black-owned business school of its kind, it was the first (private) vocational school in the nation's capital to prepare African-Americans for business and civil service. Armstrong High School had been the public "vocational" high school for Negroes.

I had been transferred to the Standards Division in the building where I worked and I was asked to be prepared to take notes at meetings of the Division chiefs, so I had to learn shorthand. The Standards Division worked closely with the Bureau of Engraving and Printing to see that items handled by the government conformed to standards. One evening at Cortez Peters a gentleman asked to speak to some of the students because he was looking for a secretary. The gentleman was Dr. Carter G. Woodson, the noted Negro historian, who had an office on Ninth Street not far from Cortez Peters Business School. He told me that he did not want to interrupt my studies or my position with the government to work for him.

Before applying to take courses at the Colored Cortez Peters Business School, I had first phoned the Washington School for Secretaries, a business school that was located in the downtown section of Washington, somewhere around Twelfth and F Streets, NW. I told the man who answered the phone that I was interested in taking speed typewriting. He said, "Sure, come right on down." Well, I went down there and when he saw me and looked at my brown skin he said, "Oh, we can't take you!" That was another of my rude introductions to Washington's way of life.

In October of 1942, Edna came to Washington to start work at the Bureau of Engraving and Printing. I told her that Martin and I had set a date to be married — Sunday, November 29, 1942. Martin and I continued with our plans and we were married at 2024 Fourth Street, NW.

The reception was held at 28 Q Street NE where Martin's brother Forrester and his family lived since their living area was a bit more spacious. My sister Edna was matron of honor. Eugene "Bud" Ford, Martin's Hampton U. classmate, was the best man. Edna's husband, Luther McIntyre and Aunt Ida came from Pennsylva-

Linda:

Cortez Peters School was the first vocational school in the nation's capital to prepare African-Americans for business and civil service. I took typing classes there during the summer when I was in Junior High School.

Cyril Crichlow had briefly owned a Business School in Harlem in the early 1920s but this school was apparently short-lived.

These business and vocational schools were an outgrowth of Booker T. Washington's philosophy of manual training. Some of us still believe these types of skills are "life skills!"

Carter G. Woodson

Cortez Peters

February Graduates of Peters Business School

February graduates of the Cortez Peters Business School in Washington. Left to right, first row, Maud Lee Mack, Ruth Lyons, Theresa Smackum, class president; Odessa Howard, Thelma D. Jones, Carrie Brooks, Melba Henderson, Gertrude Baldwin, Vashti Henderson, Ellen Dennis; second row (seated), Edith Boozer, Venora Jones, Estelle Jordan, Marietta Crichlow, Louise Heyward; third row (standing), Jean Brisco, Geraldine Nero, Margaret Clark, Mary Austin, Muriel Singletary, Norma Belle, John Dansby, Earline Davis, Annabelle Johns, Grace Savage, Agnes H. Waters, Dorothy Medley, Lettie Gilliam.—(Photo by Oscar).

The
Cortez W. Peters Business Schools
Baltimore, Md.   Chicago, Ill.   Washington, D. C.

· THIS CERTIFIES THAT ·

Marietta Louise Crichlow

has satisfactorily completed the *Shorthand*

course of study and practice in The Cortez W. Peters Business School and is therefore awarded this

Certificate

In testimony whereof we have affixed our signatures this 2th day of June 1945 at Washington, D.C.

nia to attend the ceremony. My cousin Elizabeth Johnson Lee and her husband, Clyde, had come to live in Washington in 1939. They also attended the wedding. None of my mother's relatives attended even though one of her sisters and two of her brothers lived in Washington. Martin's Aunt Rachel (Warnick) Porter came from Detroit. His uncle William Warnick came from New Jersey.

My friend Hattie had married Rev. Moses W. Beasley. He had received a degree in religion from Howard University. He was a student at Howard at the same time Hattie and I were students there. After or during the time "Beasley" (as we called him) was studying for his degree he served as Director of Religious Education at Mount Carmel Baptist Church. He performed our wedding ceremony.

Things went well that day. We had to go back to work the next day so we did not have a honeymoon. It was wartime and very few people took off from work for anything.

Martin and I received many nice gifts, some of them decorate my china cabinet to this day. One of our most useful gifts was a large enamel pot with a handle and lid that we received from a friend of Martin's mother, Ms. Bessie Winston. The pot is good for cooking large quantities of food. I have used it all through the years, and still use it many years after it was given to us. All of our gifts were and are still very much appreciated.

After the wedding, Martin came to live at 2024 Fourth Street, NW, and began to update the house. He was a master mechanic and excellent with tools. He installed a central heating system in the house and did many other kinds of repair work. He and Bud Ford built a cinder block storage shed in the backyard.

Marietta also learned the Dvorak Keyboard, which was tested during the 1940s, but was never widely adapted.

Martin and Marietta's Wedding
November 29, 1942

Wedding picture Stevens Family:
Aunt Ida Stevens Johnson, Martin,
Marietta, and John Stevens,

Wedding picture Crichlow Family:
Lillian Warnick Crichlow, Martin,
Marietta, Aunt Rachel Warnick
Porter, and Bill Warnick

SOME OF MARIETTA'S ACHIEVEMENTS

Howard University Undergraduate diploma 1941
At the time that Marietta received her Howard diplomas, they were written in Latin! Latin was the language for purely academic university diplomas at that time.

Howard University Graduate School diploma 1955

Gallaudet University Master of Science in Education 1965

In about 1964, Marietta received a fellowship to study what was then the fairly new field of Special Education at Gallaudet College in Washington. After receiving her degree in 1965 she became a special education teacher–working with, at various times, hearing impaired and visually impaired students.

POST WORLD WAR II AND A NEW BABY

Time has a way of moving on. I continued to work at Procurement and Martin worked at the Pentagon in Arlington, VA. We had a friend named Dr. Lillian G. Wheeler who in 1947 had completed her medical studies at Boston University. On August 4, 1949, Lillian was the gynecologist who delivered our baby girl, Linda. We were very pleased and excited. Aunt Ida came from Pennsylvania and visited for a few days. Edna was very helpful with it all. Linda was christened at Shiloh Baptist Church in Alexandria, Virginia, where Rev. Beasley was pastor. Lillian Wheeler was one of her godmothers.

Hattie Beasley had a little boy, William Nathaniel Beasley, born March 19, 1949. She was home taking care of her two girls and her baby. She offered to take care of Linda when I went back to work. Hattie lived on Second Street, about two blocks from where we lived. She took care of Linda for two years until we entered Linda in nursery school.

I continued to work in the Procurement Division, Treasury Department, until September of 1950, when I resigned to go back to Howard University to take some courses that I needed to qualify as a teacher. Following one year's study there in 1950 -51, I began working as a substitute teacher in the DC schools. I found this convenient because I did not have to work every day and it gave me more time at home.

In 1951, my friend, Phyllis Gibbs Fauntleroy, invited me to join a new group, the Madrecias (Mother-Daughter) Club. About the same time, our friend, Mary Jane Tyler had also asked me to join her club, Tots and Teens of DC. My child-hood friend Vivienne Scarborough had also asked me to join her club. I chose the Madrecias because Phyllis had asked me first. It was a very vibrant organization with projects for the daughters. We still have reunions. Many years later, after their children were born, Eric and Linda joined Tots and Teens; Eric, Linda, Kwame and Khalila made many life-long friends through Tots and Teens.

On August 15, 1954, a very sad thing happened. Our baby boy was stillborn at Freedmen's Hospital. But I recovered even though the experience dulled my hearing that had bothered me since about 1945. I had gone with Martin and our friend, Dr. Lillian Wheeler, to visit his mother, Lillian Crichlow, in Brandywine, Maryland, for an overnight stay. It was damp and we spent a good bit of the time out in the yard. After we returned home, the next morning when I woke up, my ears felt stopped up and I could hardly hear. Since then, I have thought that the dampness and possibly some of the plants had something to do with my hearing problem. The doctors did what they could but for several months I could not understand speech over the telephone. At work where I was required to use the telephone, things were difficult. By summer of the next year, my hearing began to clear up some, but not completely.

In 1953 I had begun to work on my master's degree in education at Howard University. I had to postpone my studies until 1955 because of my hearing problem.

In the fall of 1954 I had received an offer to teach at Kramer Junior High School in NE Washington, but had to turn it down because of my health problems. I returned to Howard University and earned my Master's degree in Education in 1956. The title of my Master's Thesis was *"The Relationship of Reading to Achievement in Certain General Education Courses."*

In 1957, I received an appointment to teach at Hine Junior High School where I taught social studies and was appointed chairman of the social studies department. One of my students at Hine, LaLeatrice Jones Hall, has kept in touch with me ever since. She had come from Miami, Florida, for one year while her mother was visiting relatives in DC. LaLeatrice has written me, phoned me, and on August 25, 2001, she came to Washington to take some courses in connection with her job in Texas and she and a friend came to visit me then. She now lives in Plano, Texas with her family.

B2 THE WASHINGTON AFRO-AMERICAN DECEMBER 26, 1998 - JANUARY 1, 1999

Courtesy Photo

MADRECIAS, Mother and Daughter Club that started 49 years ago recently got together for a bit of holiday cheer. Members (the Moms) pictured here are, down front, Arlene Shapiro, hostess; left to right: Gloria Mauney, Gwendolyn Johnson, Josephine Wade and Marietta Crichlow; Standing, Barbara Jeffries, Phyllis Fauntleroy, Carolyn Jackson, Dr. Gertrude Hunter and Texiera Nash.

THE MADRECIAS, MOTHER / DAUGHTER CLUB LUNCHEON

Members of this club, founded by the mothers of little girls 49 years ago, met recently at the home of Arlene Shapiro. The club was active for 23 years, then met only for special reunions occasions, etc. This last "reunion" was the fourth meeting at which time the mothers planned to celebrate the Golden Anniversary, with daughters ... and we hope a few good friends!

The daughters grew and developed into lovely career professionals, wives, mothers (even some grandmothers); they continued involvement in community outreach programs, as an integral part of their development and social life.

Congratulations to the Madrecias for being such good Mother/friends!

Linda: Black folks started many different clubs...for the betterment of their families and communities. One of the reasons for starting these clubs was that, prior to the late 1960s, Black folks, in some respects, didn't have the social outlets that White folks had. Interestingly, in DC especially, these social organizations and the schools and churches, with all the Black teachers, kind of insulated us from the segregation that was prevalent in most other parts of the country.

Marietta helping to give out door prizes as chair of the Howard University Women's Club amenities committee

Marietta with members of the H.U. Women's Club 2012:
l-r, Marietta, Amenities chairperson, Valerie Jordan, president; Asha Edwards, 2012 scholarship recipient; Maria Baylor, scholarship chairperson; Henrietta Capers, treasurer.

Marietta was among the first group of African-Americans to be certified to teach in the integrated DC Public Schools in 1954.

Job Offered Teacher on Merged List
The Washington Post and Times Herald (1954-1959); Jul 15, 1954;
ProQuest Historical Newspapers: The Washington Post (1877-1996)
pg. 21

First Instance

Job Offered Teacher on Merged List

District School officials have made t h e i r first offer of a teaching appointment in the public school system to a candidate on the recently merged list of white and Negro applicants.

A letter offering the appointment to an out-of-town applicant top on the list for the opening, was mailed last week. No response, however, had been received by school officials by yesterday.

It was reported the appointment offer was to fill a senior physics teacher post in Eastern High School.

Officials said additional letters offering jobs in junior high schools will be mailed out this week and a steady flow of appointments is expected to follow u n t i l the opening of school in September.

Fifty-three applicants qualified for teacher appointments in junior and vocational high schools in the first biracial tests given June 10 and 11. Officials reported 135 took the tests but pointed out that all failures were not academic but many were on the physical test given.

Successful applicants, in the order of their rating and the subjects for which they qualified, were:

COMMERCIAL ARITHMETIC AND GENERAL BUSINESS: Mrs. Thelma D. Sharper, David A. Yost.

ENGLISH: Mrs. Mary-Nona Neidlinger, Barbara A. Andreansky, Ann J. Crook, Mrs. Marion R. Flagg, Lillian M. Topalian, Mrs. Joan R. Collier, Mrs. Annie R. Jenkins, Mrs. Irene M. Wallert, Mrs. Nellie W. Lawson, Christine Glover, Mrs. Juanita L. Freeman.

FRENCH: Mrs. Marie T. Primas, Mrs. Beatrice G. Harris.

GENERAL SCIENCE: Jack E. Gillikin, Mrs. Margaret F. Saville, Harvey Wiener, Mrs. Melba B. Robinson, Mrs. Carolynne G. Branson, George Petrovich, Mrs. Lois J. Freeman, Mrs. Flora C. Ruffin, LeRoy J. Rollins, Barbara M. Thomas, Theodore P. Jenifer, Roslyn M. Wall.

GEOGRAPHY—Robert T. Williams, William P. Shook, Mrs. Julia B. King, Cynthia B. Coleman, Joan E. Dodson, Mrs. Lillie R. Head.

HISTORY — Richard C. Mattingly, Nathaniel B. Hall, Anna J. Gosnell, Mrs. Gloria W. Balkissoon, Jean A. Wilson, Mrs. Sara A. Moultrie, John R. Wheeler, Keith H. Taylor, Mrs. Marietta S. Crichlow, Mrs. Florence A. Maxwell, Woody E. Banks, Donald J. Salins, Mrs. Audrey D. Clark.

MATHEMATICS—Bernard A. Davis, Mrs. Virginia H. Tarbush, Daly I.

CHAPTER 7

My Husband, Martin A. Crichlow

Martin A. Crichlow

**Martin at Hampton
ca. 1980**

Linda: Most large cities had a "Bottom," that part of the city that started near the river banks, at the lower end of town and went into disrepair as the cities expanded northward. By the 1970s, Foggy Bottom, with the Watergate and The Kennedy Center and high-end apartments and condominiums, had become one of the more exclusive areas of Washington.

Martin Augustus Crichlow was born in Yazoo City, Mississippi, on October 7, 1912. He was the second child of Cyril Askelon Crichlow and Lillian Elizabeth Warnick Crichlow. At that time, they were missionaries for the Seventh Day Adventist Church. They left Mississippi when Martin was two years old and were living in Nashville, Tennessee, when their third child, Allwyn Forrester Crichlow, was born in 1915. The family moved around quite a bit while doing their missionary work. They lived in New York, New Jersey, and Washington, D.C.

Martin received a diploma from the Public Schools of Asbury Park, New Jersey, Grammar Department, on February 4, 1927. It was in 1927 that his parents moved to Washington, DC. They lived at 716 23rd Street, NW, in the neighborhood known as Foggy Bottom—a relatively poor neighborhood at edge of Georgetown near the river.

Martin began his high school studies at Armstrong Senior High School, located at First and M Streets, NW, and would walk with his classmates from Georgetown to First Street, NW, every school day.

Until the middle of the 1940s, Georgetown was populated largely by Colored people. During the 1940s the Colored people were urged to sell their homes and move. The White people began to move in, update the properties, and now mostly well-to-do Whites live there.

While attending high school Martin worked as an elevator operator at different buildings, delivered newspapers, and did whatever he could find to help out. He graduated from Armstrong Senior High School on January 31, 1931, and remained friends with many of his Armstrong classmates throughout the rest of his life. His class of 1931 held regular reunions, picnics, and other gatherings.

I remember Martin telling me that at the beginning of his freshman year at Hampton, he rode there from Washington, DC, with his mother's half-brother, Paul, on the back of Uncle Paul's motorcycle. While he was a student at Hampton, he lived for a while in the dormitory called "The Wigwam." As he studied, Martin also worked to earn his tuition. Some of his Armstrong High School classmates also attended Hampton. Edward Queen was one of them. Queen, as most people called him, rarely missed a reunion or a Homecoming at Hampton. Queen passed away in 2001 at his home in Washington, DC, at the age of 92.

In 1931 the United States was in the midst of a deep depression. Many people, young and old, were unable to find jobs. Soup kitchens were opened and many people stood in long lines to get food. The Civilian Conservation Corps (CCC) was organized by President Franklin Roosevelt to make it possible for young people to earn a little money.

After his freshman year, Martin joined the CCC and worked in Goshen, Virginia. It was at the CCC camp that he met George Thompson who became one of his very best friends. Martin said that at the CCC camp he told them he could type so he worked in one of the offices as company clerk. Martin's father, Cyril, had taught him how to type some years before. After a stint working in Goshen, Martin returned to Hampton and studied until the fall of 1936 when he again joined the CCC in Yorktown, Virginia. He returned to Hampton later in January of 1937 and resumed his studies. He also worked with the Works Project Administration (WPA) doing plumbing work. During this time, he stayed with his friend Chisolm Peddrew and his wife.

Vernon Gardner with his group the Deep River Boys.

He had worked helping to repair buildings on Hampton's campus to try to earn his tuition. I do not know how much his tuition was, but it was as hard to come by as tuition is today. I remember that my tuition at Howard University in 1937 was $150.00 a year plus other fees. But inflation had not yet set in. That was a lot of money back then when many people, especially women, worked eight hours a day, five days a week for private White families, and earned one dollar a day and street car fare that was ten cents one way.

Martin loved his life at Hampton and made friends that were his friends for the rest of his years. Those I met were fine people. Most of them had nicknames: Cornelius Owens was 'Big Dog," or sometimes called "C. C."; Chisolm Peddrew was "Little Dog"; Liston Baylor was "Pig"; Alonzo Griffin was "Gump"; Eugene Ford was "Bud"; and Martin was "Cris" or some called him 'Bootsie."

As I write this, all have passed on but they certainly enjoyed each other's company while they were around. Most of them ended up working in the school system and some were principals, administrators, etc. They were well thought of in the community. One of his very close Hampton classmates was Vernon Gardner who was from New York. He came to visit us several times. He sang with the Deep River Boys Quartet that traveled all over the United States and Europe. They were the contemporary of singing groups such as the Mills Brothers, a very famous quartet during the 1940s and 1950s. Martin and I attended several Hampton reunions. We attended his last reunion in 1987, before he began to ail. Even though he did not get a degree from Hampton, he was listed with the Class of 1937 and was included in the 50th anniversary picture taken with some of his classmates along with the President of Hampton, William Harvey. Martin was a staunch supporter of the University and sent contributions over the years to the Hampton Boosters Club that he had been a member of when he was a student there. He had played football and received a "letter" for playing with the team.

Martin in his Hampton "H" sweater, ca. 1985.

Hampton class of 1937, 50th year reunion. May 17, 1987. Front left, Hampton President and Mrs. William Harvey. Martin is 2nd row middle.

Bessie Fredericks, Martha Archer Crichlow Grant (Luther's widow), Lillian Crichlow Burrell (Forrester's oldest daughter), Martin, Irene Hemsley Crichlow Parker (Forrester's first wife and Allwyn Jr., and Lillian's mother), Allwyn Forrester Crichlow, Jr., Vernon Gardner. Bessie was a friend of Irene's. Photo was taken in front of Matthews Memorial Church where Allwyn was an assistant pastor, ca. 1991.

The Old Manual Training School (P Street) built in 1902

Armstrong Technical High School new building constructed in 1927. This drawing is from the yearbook.

Martin Crichlow
Armstrong 1931
yearbook

Armstrong was designed by local architect Waddy B. Wood in 1902. The Renaissance Revival building was one of two segregated manual training schools constructed for the city's African-American youth. It was named for Samuel C. Armstrong. It was dedicated by Booker T. Washington, on October 24, 1902. Students studied plumbing, carpentry, typing and other business trades but they also excelled at math, science and foreign languages. Daddy always enjoyed practicing the French he learned at Armstrong! The other manual training school was Margaret Murray (M. M.) Washington School for girls where courses such as nursing and dressmaking were taught.

Dunbar High School where Martin's brothers Luther and Forrester attended. Forrester's son Allwyn Forrester, Jr., and sister Lillian also attended Dunbar. Dunbar was renowned as the first public high school for African Americans and as an outstanding academic school. Indeed, it was a great school in its day, but Armstrong, Dunbar and Margaret Washington High schools all provided good educations back in the 1920s through 1950s. (See Alison Stewart's *First Class: The Legacy of Dunbar* for more information about both Dunbar and Armstrong.)

Martin completed grammar school in Asbury Park, NJ. He told that while still living in New Jersey with his mother, he heard of Armstrong High in Washington and wrote to his father Cyril to ask if he could stay with him in Washington and attend Armstrong.

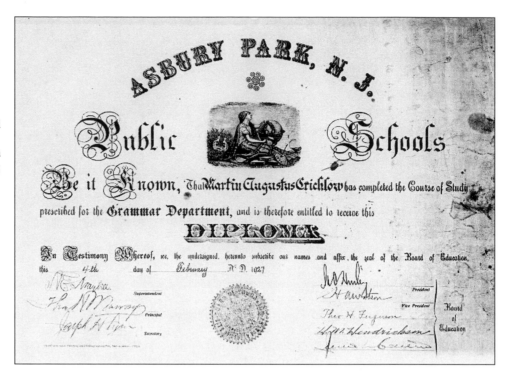

Linda note: There were large numbers of African Americans who lived in the North who moved south to places like Washington to attend segregated schools because these schools had outstanding reputations...some high schools such as Dunbar and Armstrong in Washington... and certainly the historically Black colleges and universities throughout the South.

ARMSTRONG HIGH SCHOOL
THE CITY OF WASHINGTON
DISTRICT OF COLVMBIA

Martin Augustus Crichlow

HAS HONORABLY COMPLETED THE COVRSE OF STVDY PRESCRIBED FOR THE WASHINGTON HIGH SCHOOLS

GIVEN BY AVTHORITY OF THE BOARD OF EDVCATION
OF THE DISTRICT OF COLVMBIA

IN TESTIMONY WHEREOF WE HAVE AFFIXED OVR
SIGNATVRES THIS _21st_ DAY OF _January_ 1921

PRINCIPAL OF SCHOOL

FIRST ASSISTANT
SVPERINTENDENT OF SCHOOLS

SVPERINTENDENT OF SCHOOLS

PRESIDENT BOARD OF EDVCATION

ELECTRICIANS, mechanics, plumbers and helpers employed by the Federal Works Agency have informed this column that jim-crow facilities exist in their shops in the Pentagon. They are charging also that they are victims of wholesale bias and discrimination when it comes to promotional opportunities.

Workers in these shops told me Saturday that they are forced to use separate lockers, and that white mechanics and helpers work on one side of the shop and colored on the other—and "never the twain shall meet."

Inquiry into the backgrounds of members of the group which is protesting the setup revealed that some of them hold degrees as electricians but that they are working as helpers and being given no chance for advancement. On the other hand, new recruits, always white, are being advanced speedily, even though their training may be inferior and their experience limited.

Those complaining had no objection to their names being made public, saying, "We want the higher-ups to know we are dissatisfied with the treatment we are getting. It seems we are not able to get to them any other way. Protests to our supervisors and the 'through channels' procedure seem to fall on deaf ears.

"Maybe through this method we can arouse somebody to assist us in getting the advancement opportunities we believe we rightfully deserve."

"No Opening"—White Youth Gets It

There is Randall Lee, who holds a District license as a registered electrician and has been working for FWA for two years. He graduated from A. and T. College, Greensboro, N.C., in electrical engineering. However, he can rate no better than helper in the Government although he actually performs the duties of a full-fledged electrician.

Martin Crichlow, 2024 Fourth St., N.W., a plumber for two years with the grade of CPC-6, says there have been openings in his shop for Grade 7 jobs, but the supervisor informed him there were no such openings. In the meantime a white youth who was rated a helper was promoted to the position.

He related another incident in the shop whereby a young man with a family of 10 was denied a promotion to CPC-4 because there were "no openings." A white recruit, however, was brought in as a CPC-4.

Charles English, a CPC-4 electrician's helper since 1943, says the colored helpers never get to help an electrician, unless sometimes they are sent out with members of their own race. For the most part, he adds, their job is to "put in bulbs."

The white helpers, often two and three, always go along with the electricians. When an opportunity for promotion to fill electrician vacancies comes, the minority group helpers, although they have been there longer, are always told they haven't had enough experience, he stated.

Relegated to Floor Sweepers

Darlington Jackson, 1021 49th St., N.E., a CPC-3 electrician helper, says that, in addition to putting in light bulbs, members of his race in his category are required to sweep the floor. White CPC-3 helpers are never called upon to do such menial duties, he said.

William Pinnix, 933 N St., N.W., who has been with FWA two years, says he is used as a helper but classified as a laborer. The supervisors just listen when he requests a promotion.

Daniel Faucette, 1149 Morse St., N.E., has been in the shop only four months but agreed to what the others said.

Crafton Baylous, 2046 P St., N.E., has been a plumber's helper since 1945, but often he and Crichlow do difficult jobs by themselves when they could use more help. When the white mechanics ask for additional help, they get it; but the colored mechanics are always told there's "none available."

Paging Secretary Johnson

This column is calling on Secretary of Defense Johnson to look into this jim-crowism in the Pentagon. This is certainly not in line with his announced policy of integration and equal opportunity and treatment.

I am also calling this matter to the attention of FWA Administrator Fleming and asking that he correct these evils immediately. I would also like to know where the FWA Fair Employment Committee is while these conditions are going on.

NCHA Transfers Help

There seems to be quite a bit of personnel transferring going on in the National Capital Housing Authority. William Anderson, who formerly headed the Parkside project across from Mayfair Mansions in Northeast, has been promoted and made assistant to NCHA Management Supervisor Leroy Smith at headquarters, 17th and K Sts., N.W.

Mrs. Emily P. Alexander has been elevated from assistant to Mrs. Ethel Forest at Carrollsburg in Southeast to head the Parkside project.

Mrs. Willa M. Neal, former assistant to Walter E. Washington at James Creek Syphax-Anthony Bowen, was moved to Carrollsburg to replace Mrs. Alexander.

A new recruit, Mrs. Carlie Adams, 4408 E St., S.E., former Treasury Department employee but more recently just a plain housewife, replaces Mrs. Neal.

The Washington Afro-American, July 2, 1949

Martin A. Crichlow, CPC-6 plumber in the Pentagon Group of Federal Works Agency—Public Buildings Administration filed discrimination charges with the Fair Employment Board recently.

Mr. Crichlow stated in his complaint that two CPC-7 positions for steamfitter were open; that his name, along with those of three others, was submitted for the post. The two others, both of whom were white, were hired and he was not although he has seniority as an employee of FWA-PBA over them, he complains.

When he asked how this came about, it was explained that they had more experience in the trade than Crichlow and were hired on the basis of experience rather than seniority.

Mr. Crichlow takes the position that by this line of reasoning he might be employed by PHA for 15 or 20 years while some other person with less tenure of service in the agency but with longer experience at the plumbing trade, would be entitled to a promotion before he would. He feels this is not consistent with fair employment policies. He says that he believes that he is being discriminated against.

Board Backs FWA Personnel

The FWA Fair Employment Board wrote Mr. Crichlow, Thursday upholding the department's opinion. It pointed out that Crichlow was not considered for the steamfitter job this time because he had turned down two previous promotions for steamfitter posts.

Crichlow explains that he is not the only one that has turned down such jobs as were offered at that time. The positions were in hot steam ducts and the only reason they were offered ____ace was because all of the white plumbers eligible would not accept them because of the danger involved.

This column has to go along with Mr. Crichlow in the belief that, regardless of what excuse FWA gives for its action, it is a case of discrimination.

If Mr. Crichlow were the only person making such complaints about FWA practices we might be inclined to say the agency is just stretching a point. However, several workers in the plumbing, electrical and mechanical shops have made similar complaints about the lack of promotional opportunities there.

Discrimination Wide Spread

Perhaps FWA's fair employment board can explain why colored electricians mates are only allowed to put in light bulbs and when a vacancy occurs the white electricians mates who are permitted to accompany the electricians on their jobs invariably get the elevated position "because they have had more experience."

Or maybe the FEP Board can explain why the colored electricians and mechanics are forced to sweep floors while the whites in the same grades are not; or why the colored semiskilled craftsmen can work only with their own race—a practice which is used against them when the agency has a higher position they might be eligible to fill.

This column must also agree with Mr. Crichlow that either the Government has a seniority system or it doesn't. The Civil Service policy, and what is supposed to be that of each agency, is to promote from within wherever possible. The main factors in considering eligibility are ability to do the work, seniority and efficiency ratings. Crichlow's ratings in this instance stack up with the other two; he has been in FWA longer than either of the others, and has proved on numerous occasions, that he can do the work. What more is required.

Whether FWA or its FEP Board wants to admit it or not, this column believes they have just been caught with their prejudice up.

These are two clippings from 1949 describing discrimination in the General Services Administration. However, by 1955, Martin was made Assistant Supervisor and by 1956 or so he became the first (as far as we know) African American Plumbing Foreman in the Washington area General Services Administration (GSA). In this position, it was his responsibility to install and maintain all of the plumbing and heating systems at the old Navy and Munitions Buildings, and some other nearby buildings. The Navy and Munitions Buildings were "temporary" buildings.

In 2013, Linda attended a meeting of the African American Historical and Genealogical Society and met Elizabeth Jean Brumfield. Elizabeth had written a book about her stepfather, Dudley Brumfield, a plumber who had to fight to get into the plumber's union in Pittsburgh back in the 1950s. Like Daddy, he had to fight to receive equal treatment. However, because Daddy worked in the government, he did not have to join a union but I do remember Daddy talking about the discriminatory nature of the unions. Elizabeth titled her book An Ordinary Man: Black Power in Overalls. *Indeed African Americans in all walks of life had to fight for their rights. It is fortunate for us that our ancestors stood their ground. And Elizabeth and Linda are trying to make sure that their stories don't go "down the drain."*

GENERAL SERVICES ADMINISTRATION

Region 3
Washington 25, D. C.
November 7, 1958

IN REPLY REFER TO: 3HPR

Mr. Martin A. Crichlow
West Area
Buildings Management Division
Public Buildings Service

Dear Mr. Crichlow:

The Regional Incentive Awards Committee has reviewed and approved the justification recommending you for a Special Service Award.

I am pleased to inform you that a cash award in the amount of $100.00 has been granted you in recognition of your performance under the provisions of Title III, Public Law 763, 83d Congress. This award, of course, is subject to income tax deductions.

Sincerely yours

H. P. Johnson
Chairman
Regional Incentive Awards Committee

GENERAL SERVICES ADMINISTRATION

Region 3
Washington 25, D. C.
August 26, 1958

IN REPLY REFER TO: 3PBM

FOR PERSONAL DELIVERY

CRICHLOW, Martin A.
WB-21, Plumber-Steamfitter Foreman
Navy Group

Dear Sir:

I wish to take this opportunity to express to you how much I appreciate the splendid cooperation and assistance you rendered the Bureau of Ships in constructing a Polaris Program Management Center.

The excellent cooperation and workmanship that was largely responsible for the expedition of this work was observed and brought to our attention by Rear Admiral J. M. Farrin, Special Assistant to Chief of Bureau for Polaris Shipbuilding Program.

Admiral Farrin mentioned that this work was done on short notice with an extremely close deadline for its completion. Through your cooperativeness and wise employment of the skills of the men under your supervision, this work was completed in record time. Also, in some instances when skilled men were not available you performed the necessary tasks to keep the work moving.

I extend to you Admiral Farrin's personal thanks as he requested and add my appreciation for your ability in guiding and supervising the men so efficiently as to bring forth a letter of appreciation on the workmanship of this assignment. I commend you for your ability in this instance and trust that you will continue with this type of supervision and services in all future assignments.

A copy of both this letter and the memorandum from Admiral Farrin will be placed in your personal folder. There is attached a copy of Admiral Farrin's memorandum for your information and records.

Sincerely yours

W. B. Montgomery
Manager, West Area

Enclosure

Martin Crichlow in the Plumbing Supervisor's office.

Despite the discrimination of the 1940s, as described in the Afro-American news articles (page 79), according to later documentation, Daddy was not only a higher pay grade but was foreman by 1958. He received numerous commendations for his work over the years. Daddy enjoyed his work; he used to often send for me to spend a couple of hours on the job with him. He'd take me around to all the offices and introduce me to the other folks who worked in his building. I remember that they were always very nice to me and seemed to think highly of him.

Paul Underwood,
Assistant Supervisor

Hattie, Martin, Marietta with friends on the Howard University Campus, ca. 1942

Martin and I would go to the Lincoln, Howard, and/or Republic theaters from time to time. The years passed and I continued my studies at Howard. Martin and 'Bud" Ford would stop by and we would play board games from time to time. On some Saturday mornings, Martin would meet some of my friends and me at Banneker playground at Georgia Avenue and Euclid Streets, NW, and play tennis. I have a picture of the four of us taken on the Banneker tennis court—Jane Diggs, Evelyn Green, Martin, and me.

Martin had been working for various plumbers, a trade that he had studied at Hampton. He returned to Hampton during 1939 and worked on a project there for a year or so. Hampton was mostly a trade school when he was a college student there during the 1930s. His male classmates majored in bricklaying, auto mechanics, carpentry and the like. The girls majored in teaching or nursing.

Martin had worked for a while in Washington, DC, with a plumber, Watha T. Daniels. There is a D.C. library at 8th Street and Rhode Island Avenue, NW, in the Shaw neighborhood, named in honor of Mr. Daniels, a community activist and one of the first African American licensed plumbers.

In 1940 Martin received an appointment to work as a plumber at the Veterans Administration. He enjoyed his work there. Often his White supervisor, Mr. Grigsby, would come to him to ask for help in solving plumbing problems that Mr. Grigsby did not know how to handle. Martin was better equipped and more skillful than most others. In 1949, with the help of his good friend, Attorney John D. Fauntleroy, Martin applied to the Fair Employment Practice Commission to appeal the government's failure to give him a promotion. After many conferences and legal correspondence, he received a promotion, and in a few years he was made assistant supervisor of plumbing at the Pentagon. It was an unusual appointment because Colored folks weren't given supervisory jobs in those days. He seemed to get along with his co-workers, even the White ones.

In about 1955, Martin was transferred to the Navy Department building at 21st and Constitution Avenue, NW, and became a plumbing supervisor, the first Black plumbing supervisor in the General Services Administration (GSA). Some years later, one of the White workers who succeeded Martin after he had been promoted to another position at Van Ness General Services Bldg in Washington, stopped by our house. He said that often when he had plumbing problems at the Pentagon, he would ask himself "Now how would Mr. Crichlow handle this?"

After he bought a car, and until I started to drive and bought a car in 1965, Martin would drive Edna and me and later Linda to Sunday school and come back for us almost every Sunday. He had been raised by very religious parents but he was not a "churchy" person himself. He would attend church programs only occasionally.

Martin was always an expert with tools. Shortly after we married, he installed a new gas heating system at 2024 4th Street, NW, and did lots of other needed improvements. We would go to the movies some Sunday evenings at the Republic, Howard, or Lincoln theaters. We socialized with friends going to house parties

Even though Martin did not finish Hampton, he loved his "Home by the Sea"
and supported the school financially.
Pictured here are Velma Patterson, Martin and Marietta at one of the Hampton Century Fund
dinners, 1966. Mrs. Patterson was the wife of another of Daddy's Hampton classmates.

The D. C. Chapter of
The Hampton Alumni Association
requests the pleasure of your company
at our
Second Annual Century Fund Dinner
Saturday evening, February 26, 1966
Washington Hilton
Conn. Ave. and Columbia Rd., N. W.
Crystal Suite - East and West

Reception 7 p. m.
Black Tie

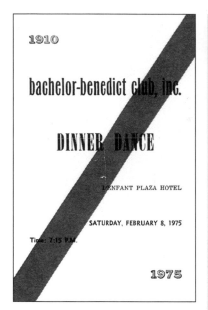

Bachelor Benedict inductees, 1967. Martin is first row, left.

Martin and Marietta did find time to socialize a bit. Martin joined the Bachelor Benedicts in 1967. According to their website, "due to the prevailing social atmosphere, brought about by the aftermath of the American Civil War (1861-1865), many area citizens were subjected to treatment that sponsored discrimination and disfranchisement. Along with churches, many beneficial and relief organizations were established to aid the District's destitute. Subsequently, as well, several social clubs were established with the intent to promote family reconstruction, to awaken social awareness and encourage positive values throughout the community. Our Club was dedicated to these goals."
Bachelor Benedicts was formed in 1910 and still exists in 2013."

Martin and Marietta dressed for another Bachelor Benedict event

and other functions. We traveled quite a bit. We took cruises to Bermuda and to various islands in the Caribbean. We went on a very nice trip to Mexico. Linda went with us.

We visited Mexico City, Guadalajara, and Acapulco in 1974. We took trips with the AARP and other groups to Niagara Falls, to Canada and to places in New York State. All were enjoyable. During the 1960s, most summers we went to Martha's Vineyard and stayed with Pauline and Frontiss Newton of D.C. who had a home there on Vineyard Haven. Martha's Vineyard consists of several islands —Edgartown, Chappaquiddick, Vineyard Haven, and Oaks Bluff. So, it was not all work. We grabbed some pleasure in between. Our trips to Hampton were always enjoyable. One summer, Martin went back to Mexico and California with George Thompson and other friends. I did not go on that trip.

Shortly after Martin and I were married I found out that he had stomach problems. The doctor said it was a duodenal ulcer. He had to be very careful with what he ate and drank. All through the years he would get stomach upsets. It was in 1965 that his doctor recommended surgery. He had two-thirds of his stomach removed. After this, his stomach problems improved. He retired from the General Services Administration in 1972 and received an award for 31 years of loyal service.

He seemed to enjoy his retirement. He was good at carpentry, electricity, and

84

Linda: The Republic, Howard and Lincoln Theaters were on U Street—Black Broadway in DC back in the 1920s through the early 1960s. The Howard Theater featured stage shows showcasing stars like Duke Ellington, Moms Mabley, Count Basie and later the Motown Review! In 1965 we could see the entire Motown Review for about $5.00!

general repair work and continued this work after retiring from the G.S.A. In 1982 he remodeled the kitchen at 543 Randolph Street where we lived. To this day, many people remark about what a good job he did. Over the many years since we moved to Randolph Street he had remodeled the basement, the baths, and other rooms. I often wished we had bought a detached house in another area. We looked around, but Martin was reluctant to move. His family had moved many, many times when he was growing up and I guess that was enough for him.

In 1984, he began to complain again. In December of that year he had surgery for cancer of the colon. From that time, he was not 100%. In 1987 he lost a good bit of weight and began to feel weak. The doctor said that his food was not being digested properly. In 1988 he was very ill in Providence Hospital. The doctors decided to put him on intravenous feedings. From 1988 for the remainder of his life, he received intravenous feedings at night for several hours every night. The nurses taught me how to handle it. For a few years he did fairly well but in 1991 he began to fail. On the morning of September 22, 1992, he died at home. He had been put under hospice care a few months before. The nurse was here when he passed.

He and several of his friends had said they wanted their bodies cremated. Alonzo Griffin and some others were cremated, as was Martin. His funeral was held at Mount Carmel Baptist Church on September 26, 1992. His nephew, the Reverend Allwyn Forrester Crichlow, gave the eulogy. On October 7, 1995, a service was held and his remains were placed beside those of his mother at Rock Creek Cemetery, Second and Webster Streets, NW, at Rock Creek Church Road, NW, Lot 127, Section 5, block 5. Headstones had been set up there for both of them. I will be placed in the same block. Space for other family members has been purchased at the same section.

Acapulco 1974

CHAPTER 8
THE BEASLEYS
OUR LIFE-LONG FRIENDS

When I enrolled as a freshman at Howard, my childhood playmate, Almarian Stoakley who lived across the street from me, also enrolled. A day or two after the beginning of the school year in 1937, Almarian introduced me to a friend of hers named Hattie Walton who, along with Almarian, attended Mount Carmel Baptist Church. This was the beginning of a long, close friendship that lasted until Hattie passed away on July 10, 2001.

It was Hattie who invited me to go with her and her family one Sunday to Mount Carmel, located at 901 Third Street, NW. This was really very strange. There are dozens of Colored churches in Washington, DC, but she invited me to Mount Carmel.

**Hattie with Pudney,
ca. 1950**

Hattie lived at 1715 Fourth Street, NW, with her mother, Mrs. Louise Meachum, her step-father, Mr. Meachum, and her half-sister, Frances. While walking to her classes at Howard, Hattie would frequently stop by my house and we would walk together up the hill to Howard.

Hattie was pianist for the Sunday school at Mt. Carmel. She would sometimes come and play the piano that had belonged to my mother, where I lived on Fourth Street. One day on the campus, Hattie introduced me to Martha Archer who was a senior at Howard. Martha received her degree in June of 1938 and married Martin's older brother, Luther, in November of 1938.

Hattie introduced me to many new friends: among them were Gertrude Payne and Avonia Williams. One day Hattie said that a few of her friends who lived near her were coming to her house that afternoon. She asked me to come down to her house and meet them. One of the young people that I met that day was Martin Crichlow.

Hattie had introduced me to Martin and Eugene (Bud) Ford in early 1938. Shortly afterward, Martin returned to Hampton to work on a project there. After a year or so, he returned to Washington, DC, and lived with his father on Oakdale Street, NW. I think the address was 337. I was a freshman at Howard when I met him. Bud, Hattie and I would socialize from time to time. They were not 'boyfriends' of hers, just friends. We would play board games or talk on the front porch. Martin's family were neighbors of Hattie. She lived at 1715 Fourth Street, NW. Martin had previously lived with his mother and younger brother at Fourth and R Streets, NW. Hattie was a very friendly person. She introduced me to several of her friends at Mt. Carmel Baptist Church. Her mother and step-father were very nice and made me feel at home whenever I visited them.

My friend Hattie had married Rev. Moses W. Beasley who had received a degree in religion from Howard University. He was a student at Howard at the same time Hattie and I were students there. After or during the time "Beasley" (as we called him) was studying for his degree he served as Director of Religious Education at Mount Carmel Baptist Church. He performed our wedding ceremony.

Hattie and Beasley had two daughters—Louise born in 1939 and Jacqueline in 1941—and had a little boy, William Nathaniel Beasley, born March 19, 1949. She was home taking care of her two girls and her baby. She offered to take care of Linda when I went back to work. Hattie lived on Second Street, about two blocks from where we lived. She took care of Linda for two years until I entered Linda in nursery school.

Martin's co-worker who drove him to work at the Pentagon would pick up Linda and Martin, drop her off at Hattie's house, then he and Martin would go on to work. Linda seemed to enjoy the company of Hattie's little boy, William (Pudney).

When Linda was about 6 months old, she was christened by Rev. Beasley at his church, Shiloh Baptist, in Alexandria where he had been appointed about 1948. Later Beasley performed the marriage ceremony for Linda and also christened Eric and Linda's children, Kwame and Khalila, continuing the tradition.

We—Marietta, Martin, Hattie, and Beasley—remained life-long friends. And now that Hattie and Beasley have passed on, we are friends with their children and grandchildren.

Marietta with Louise and Jackie Beasley, ca. 1948.

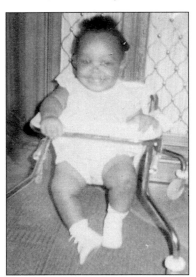

Marietta and Martin were named godparents of Hattie and Beasley's granddaughter Jeanette in 1968. (daughter of Jackie and John Darden).

The Beasleys help Martin and Marietta celebrate their 25th Wedding anniversary, 1967. l-r: Linda, Edna, Hattie Beasley, Rev. Moses W. Beasley, Marieta, Martin

Jeanette Darden Johnson with husband Reggie and children Amy, John and Alysha, ca. 2008.

Will Appear In Recital

REV. MOSES W. BEASLEY, Tenor

Who will appear in recital at the Mt. Lebanon Baptist Church, Thursday evening, May 8 at eight-thirty p.m. under the sponsorship of the Women's Club of the church. Proof of the exceptional quality of Reverend Beasley's finely trained voice can be found in the many requests made each year by leading Washington churches and colleges throughout the South where he appears as guest artist and at Easter and Christmas sings the tenor role in Cantatas and Oratorios such as Mendelssohn's "Elijah" or Handel's "Messiah."

For two years Rev. Beasley appeared with the National Negro Opera Company at the Water Gate, Washington, D.C.; at the Chicago Opera House; Syria Mosque, Pittsburgh, Pa.; Madison Square Garden and at Town Hall with the New York Opera Guild.

Rev. Beasley is assistant to the pastor, Dr. W. H. Jernagin, Mt. Carmel Baptist Church where he is in charge of the Youth Church and is Director of the Gospel Chorus. Among his many other affiliations are: Assistant Director, Public Appearance Chanters of Columbia Lodge No. 85 Elks; recording secretary, Washington, D.C. Branch of the National Alliance of Postal Employees; treasurer, Alumni Association of the School of Religion, Howard University; member of Mu Lambda Chapter, Alpha Phi Alpha Fraternity; the Washington Federation of Churches, the Federal Council of Churches of America and other progressive organizations.

He is a native of Memphis, Tennessee where he began his singing career as a boy soprano at the age of five. In later years he became known to Baptists throughout the nation as the "Song Bird of the South," serving at one time as assistant to the Director of Music of the National B.T.U. & S.S. Congress. For eight consecutive years he was a featured artist on Memphis radio station WNBR.

At Lane College, Rev. Beasley studied Music and Voice under Miss C. N. Stephens and the late Prof. I. J. Berry. As leading tenor in the Lane College Choral Society he made annual tours throughout the middle west; he was once offered a position with the Ford Eight of Detroit, but chose to remain at Lane College. Upon coming to Washington he entered the School of Religion, Howard University, where he studied under Count DeVermond and became affiliated with the University Glee Club with which he had the honor to sing

SOUVENIR PROGRAM

First Annual Music and Dance Festival

SATURDAY, JULY 19, 1947

8:30 P. M.

Griffith Stadium

Sponsored By

THE WASHINGTON GUILDS
of
THE NATIONAL
NEGRO OPERA CO., Inc.

Dr. Jesse A. Keene
General Chairman

Mary Cardwell Dawson
Managing Director

SPECIAL FEATURE:
Princess Consulo Nyoko Exotic Interpricione of Tropical Danseuse

MASTER OF CEREMONIES:
Reginald Franklin Fisher

MOSES BEASLEY
Tenor

Rev. Beasley was an outstanding tenor who performed with the National Negro Opera Company

This event was held about one and one-half years before King was assassinated on April 4, 1968 in Memphis, Tennessee.

Martin Luther King, Jr., and Rev. Beasley at the sixtieth anniversary celebration of the founding of Alpha Phi Alpha Fraternity, Inc. December 3, 1966.

Mu Lambda Chapter
of
Alpha Phi Alpha Fraternity, Inc.
Washington, D. C.

The Sixtieth Anniversary Celebration

of the founding of

Alpha Phi Alpha Fraternity, Inc.

Saturday, December 3, 1966
Washington Hilton International Ballroom

Dr. Henry A. Callis
Honoree

Dr. Martin Luther King, Jr.
Principal Speaker

Rev. Beasley, Hattie and Martin at Alpha Phi Alpha event in 1966

Both MLK and Rev. Beasley were Alphas. Marietta, Martin, and Linda attended this event with Rev. Beasley, Marietta, Hattie, and Pudney.

CHAPTER 9

CYRIL ASKELON CRICHLOW FATHER OF MARTIN A. CRICHLOW

Cyril Crichlow ca. 1940

Cyril Askelon Crichlow was the only child of Samuel Augustus Crichlow and Agnes Louise Crichlow. I do not know her maiden name. Cyril was born in Trinidad, British West Indies on September 12, 1889. His father was born in Port-of-Spain, Trinidad, British West Indies in the year 1858 and died on June 8, 1929, at 71 years of age. Samuel Crichlow had worked in real estate on the island. Samuel's mother was Rebecca Pilgrim. I do not have any other information about Cyril Crichlow's parents.

Cyril Crichlow had attended the public schools in Trinidad and was sent to the United States in about 1904 when he was 15 years old. He enrolled at Union College in Lincoln, Nebraska. Union College was a Seventh Day Adventist institution. It was at that school where he learned more about the fundamentals of the Bible. According to some sources, he attended Meharry Medical College in Nashville, Tennessee, but did not complete his studies there. Cyril spoke with very good diction. *[Linda: As children, we Crichlow grandchildren thought Grandpop spoke "proper." We didn't realize until much later that he was speaking with a British West Indian accent. Even though we always knew he was from Trinidad, we really didn't know about the people and culture of Trinidad.]*

Lillian, Cyril and youngest child Forrester, ca. 1919

On May 30, 1909, Cyril Crichlow married Lillian Elizabeth Warnick. The marriage ceremony was performed in Mobile, Alabama. They were missionaries of the Seventh Day Adventist Church and traveled from place to place. Their first two children, Luther and Martin, were born in Yazoo City, Mississippi. Their youngest child, Allwyn Forrester, was born in Nashville, Tennessee. Martin had told me that the family also had lived in Huntsville, Alabama; Anniston, Alabama; New York, New York; Brooklyn, New York; Newark, Jersey City, Bound Brook, and Asbury Park, New Jersey; and in several locations in Washington, D.C.

In 1918, Cyril Crichlow served with the American Expeditionary Forces in France and Germany during World War I. Records show that in 1921 he was secretary to Marcus Garvey, who during the 1920s was working toward encouraging the Colored people in the United States to return to Liberia, Africa, to set up a free state. Garvey's organization was the United Negro Improvement Association—UNIA. With another gentleman, Cyril Crichlow set up a business school in New York City on Seventh Avenue—Crichlow-Braithwaite Shorthand School. He was an expert typist. See copy of an advertisement for the school on page 92.

The family was living in Asbury Park, New Jersey, when Cyril moved to Washington, DC, to take a job as mail handler at the Munitions Building, Department of the Army. Six months later his wife, Lillian Crichlow, came to Washington with the children. They lived at 716 23rd Street, NW. In 1930 Cyril and Lillian Crichlow were divorced. He later married again and subsequently divorced again. Government personnel records indicate that in 1938, Cyril was a messenger in the War Department. A 1039 service rating form cited his work site as *War Department, Air Corps Bureau, Mail and Record Division.* By 1944, his position was "clerk." In 1950 he was "mail clerk," His 1950 efficiency rating was "excellent." Indeed, Cyril had excellent writing and typing skills and in another era would have qualified for a different type of job.

Miss Van

Cyril Crichlow wrote several religious treatises. In 1956 his book, *The New Birth, a Bible Study in Spiritual Biology,* was published by Pageant Press, Inc., 130 West 42nd Street, New York, New York. In this book he aimed to explain the scriptures as he understood them. He also had published other religious writings such as: "The Harmony of the Resurrection." published in November, 1929, and the "Feast of Pentecost." He was an evangelist and promotion director for the Christian Fellowship of the World. At one time during the latter part of his life, he held services at his residence for a group called "The Gatherers."

About 1941 Cyril Crichlow married a nurse, Caroline Van Husen, a White lady who had been a resident of New York City. After she came to Washington, DC, they lived at 300 T Street, NW. In addition to his religious activities, Cyril also liked opera and classical music. One of his hobbies was listening to recordings of classical musicians.

Martin's father had some cousins. One was Rita Haynes who lived in New York City. Martin and I visited her at her home in New York many years ago. I wish I had inquired more about their family's history. Cyril Crichlow also had a cousin named John F. Crichlow who lived at 818 Tulip Avenue, Knoxville, Tennessee, and was 93 years old in 1958. According to correspondence, John was not very well at that time.

Cyril, World War I

Cyril Crichlow began to ail during his later years with a heart problem and diabetes. He passed away on February 20, 1965. Funeral services were held on February 25, 1965, at the Fort Meyer Chapel in Arlington, Virginia. He was buried at Arlington National Cemetery. Miss Van, as many called his third wife, passed away on January 3, 1977, at Washington Hospital Center. Her burial was at Arlington Memorial Cemetery.

Thanks to our cousin Donna Crichlow, in the early 2000s, years after Cyril's death in 1965, we learned much more about our grandfather's experiences with Marcus Garvey. He actually had been Garvey's resident commissioner in Liberia.

CRICHLOW-BRAITHWAITE SHORTHAND SCHOOL

"THE SCHOOL OF MERIT"

CLASSES NOW ORGANIZING. ENROLL TODAY.

COURSES

SHORTHAND	TYPEWRITING	BOOKKEEPING
COURT REPORTING	GENERAL REPORTING	SECRETARIAL SUBJECTS
COMMERCIAL LAW	BUSINESS METHODS	CIVIL SERVICE
REGENTS EXAMINATIONS	PREPARATORY COURSES	ARITHMETIC
ALGEBRA	GEOMETRY	TRIGONOMETRY
GRAMMAR	COMPOSITION	SPELLING
PENMANSHIP	SPANISH	FRENCH
LATIN	GREEK	ETC.

DAY AND EVENING CLASSES

The CRICHLOW-BRAITHWAITE Shorthand School is the leading Colored Business School in New York City. Its teaching staff consists of persons unquestionably the peers in their respective fields. In the field of Stenography Messrs. Crichlow and Braithwaite need no introduction to the general public. They are not merely theoretical teachers, they are practical professional shorthand writers who, as in the past, will continue to teach their students the most successful and practical way of studying and writing shorthand. Pitmanic System only taught. We secure positions for all our competent graduates. Diplomas and certificates given for all courses. Correspondence course in Shorthand to all parts of the world. Write for particulars. Phone Audubon 1390.

CYRIL A. CRICHLOW   **I. NEWTON BRAITHWAITE**

2376 SEVENTH AVENUE, AT WEST 139th STREET

Crichlow-Braithwaite typing school
students

Cyril with co-workers at the War Department ca. 1950. Government personnel records indicate that in 1938, Cyril was a messenger in the War Department. A 1039 service rating form cited his work site as War Department, Air Corps Bureau, Mail and Record Division. By 1944, his position was "clerk." In 1950 he was "mail clerk," His 1950 efficiency rating was "excellent." Indeed, Cyril had excellent writing and typing skills and in another era would have qualified for a different type of job.

CYRIL CRICHLOW AND MARCUS GARVEY

The previous material on Cyril was written in the 1990s by Marietta. Following is a more recent "biography" written by Dr. Robert Hill, Professor Emeritus of UCLA. Dr. Hill was the curator of the Marcus Garvey Archives at UCLA who visited us in Washington after our cousin Donna Crichlow e-mailed him with questions. Prior to Donna contacting him, Dr. Hill had no idea that Cyril had descendants living. He thought Cyril had "dropped out" of the West Indian community (in New York) and Hill lost track of him. In a way, Cyril had dropped out—he moved to DC and got his GGJ (good government job) and had nothing else to do with Garvey as far as we know.

Cyril Askelon Crichlow

Cyril Askelon Crichlow (1889-1965), World War I veteran, schoolteacher, missionary, business and secretarial school principal, court reporter, evangelist, religious writer, and government employee, was the UNIA** official reporter and reporter to the UNIA convention. He was born in Port-of-Spain, Trinidad, into a highly religious family, from whom, he claimed, "he inherited his unquenchable faith as well as his curiosity to probe deeper into the mysteries locked within the scriptures," recalling that from early on he possessed "an unquenchable yearning for the higher—in fact, what might be called the celestial things of life, especially as concerning the cultural aspects and most importantly the spiritual values . . . instilled into the very warp and woof of my being by God-fearing parents" (Cyril A. Crichlow, "About the Author" and "Biographical Sketch," Appendix I, The New Birth: A Handbook of Scriptural Documentation [New York: Pageant Press, 1956], 134).

After eight years of common schooling, he attended the Government Training School in Trinidad, 1900-1905. At the age of fifteen, he was sent to the U.S. to study at Union College, in Lincoln, Nebraska, a Seventh Day Adventist missionary institution, in preparation for a career as a medical missionary. He attended Union College, 1905-1908, graduating from the academy in May 1908 (academy was the term used for high school work, since the college was only just beginning). Upon graduation, he served in the South as a missionary and teacher; from 1908-1913, he taught school in Mississippi and Alabama.

In October 1917, while attending Meharry Medical College in Nashville, Tennessee, he enlisted in the U.S. Army. He served with the American Expeditionary Force in France, with the rank of sergeant first class, as a clerk in the Surgeon's Office, 92nd Division. He was decorated with the Victory Button (Bronze) and Victory Medal with Battle Clasps. After he was demobilized in March 1919, he was employed from April 1919 through February 1920 as a clerk with the Post Office Department, New York City (Foreign Station—Christopher Street). In 1919, Crichlow applied for and became a naturalized U.S. citizen.

In 1920, Crichlow attended the City College of New York, where he studied high speed shorthand and court reporting. That summer, together with I. Newton Braithwaite, he established the "Crichlow-Braithwaite Shorthand School," in Harlem. He was employed by the UNIA at this time as its official reporter and served as a member of the UNIA executive council. The following year, in January 1921, he was engaged by Garvey who appointed him "Resident Secretary" of the UNIA commissariat in Liberia, at a salary of $2500 a year, with responsibility "for all our records and all data and reports pertaining to the interests of the Universal Negro Improvement Association in Liberia".

Effectively, Crichlow was the business manager and auditor of the UNIA technical team despatched to Liberia in 1921 for the purpose of carrying out "the Construction Work and upbuilding of Liberia through the program of the Universal Negro Improvement Association" (DNA, RG 59, File 882.00/705, Marcus Garvey to High Highness the Hon. Gabriel Johnson, Monrovia, Liberia, February 1, 1921).

Crichlow arrived in Liberia on 18 March 1921, but by the following month found himself at odds with the UNIA Potentate Gabriel Johnson, who was also the mayor of Monrovia, and the Supreme Deputy Potentate, George O. Marke, over the proper administration of funds and the distribution of authority over the affairs

93

of the UNIA commisariat. He received his wages for the months of February, March, and April, but after relations with the Potentate became severely strained, it being alleged that he tried to usurp the power of the Potentate, payment of his wages was suspended.

Destitute and extremely sick as a result of blackwater fever, Crichlow appealed to the American legation, in April 1921, for assistance. The American resident minister, Joseph L. Johnson, exploited the opportunity presented by Crichlow's extremity to extract from him a substantial cache of confidential documents bearing on the activities of the UNIA in Liberia, documents which were then forwarded to the U.S. State Department in Washington, D.C. ("The Legation at once took advantage of this opportunity to secure all papers and possible information covering the Organization and its work," DNA, RG 59, file 882.00/705, Joseph L. Johnson, Minister Resident, Monrovia, Liberia, to the Secretary of State, Washington, D.C., 16 July 1921, with attachments).

Crichlow finally sailed from Monrovia on 6 August; he arrived in New York, after a brief stopover in Spain, on 11 September 1921. He resigned officially from the UNIA a few days later, on 15 September, but not before he presented a claim for $1237 for unpaid salary and traveling and other expenses in connection with his services in Liberia as Resident Secretary, together with the cost of his passage from Liberia to New York, but it was refused, whereupon he sued the UNIA.

On 26 January 1922, a court and jury in New York issued a verdict in favor of Crichlow and awarded him $700 of his original claim ("Court and Jury Deny Full Claim of U.N.I.A. Ex-Employe for Wages—Non-Performance of Service Proved," NW, 4 February 1922). Joining the rival African Blood Brotherhood, in De-

cember 1921 he published "What I Know about Liberia," criticizing Garvey in Briggs's Crusader magazine (Crusader 5, no. 4 [December 1921]: 20—23; 6, no. 1 [January—February 1922]: 18—23; MGP 1—4).

Crichlow lived for a time in Asbury Park, New Jersey, and traveled as a missionary with the Seventh Day Baptist Church (his two oldest children were born in Yazoo City, Mississippi, and his youngest son was born in West Virginia). From 1927 until retirement, due to disability, in 1951, he was employed continuously with the federal government in Washington, D.C. His final position was with the correspondence control branch of the Secretary of the Air Staff Executive Division, U.S. Air Force.

Much of his spare time during these years was spent conducting research at the Library of Congress, and conducting evangelistic work with the Christian Fellowship of the World, in Washington, D.C. During these years, he published numerous works on regeneration theology, culminating in the publication of *The New Birth*. Other works included *The Triune Name* (Washington, DC: The Christian Fellowship of the World, 1934), *The Baptismal Name* (New York: Unification Association, 1960), and several pamphlets, among them "The Harmony of the Resurrection," "The Harmony of Visits to the Sepulcher," "The Feast of Pentecost," "The Godhead a Dualism, not a Trinity," and other writings. He is buried in Arlington National Cemetery (Crichlow Family Papers, Washington, D.C.; U.S. Civil Service Commission, Washington, D.C., Service Record of Cyril A. Crichlow; Sabrina Riley, director, Union College Library, to Prof. Robert A. Hill, 24 November 2003; 12 December 2003).

Cyril Crichlow, seated front right, with members of UNIA

Linda note: These cards and letter were part of Nana's (Lillian W. Crichlow) papers. She had held on to them, through the 1933 divorce, through moving to many locales and through a house fire. She gave them to me after my first trip to Africa in 1971 with Operation Crossroads Africa. When I returned from Ghana that summer, Aunt Martha said to me, "You're trying to be like your grandfather; he went to Africa with Marcus Garvey." Well, prior to that, I had never heard of him going to Africa. No one ever discussed it. And, really, I didn't pursue the topic much even then. It wasn't until 2003 when cousin Donna Crichlow contacted Dr. Robert Hill at UCLA that we knew the extent of his involvement with Garvey. Having learned that Cyril had actually been a government witness against Garvey, I believe that, just as today, when government witnesses are often sworn to secrecy, Grandpop must have agreed to not discuss his involvement with Garvey.

In addition, he might have actually regretted the entire affair.

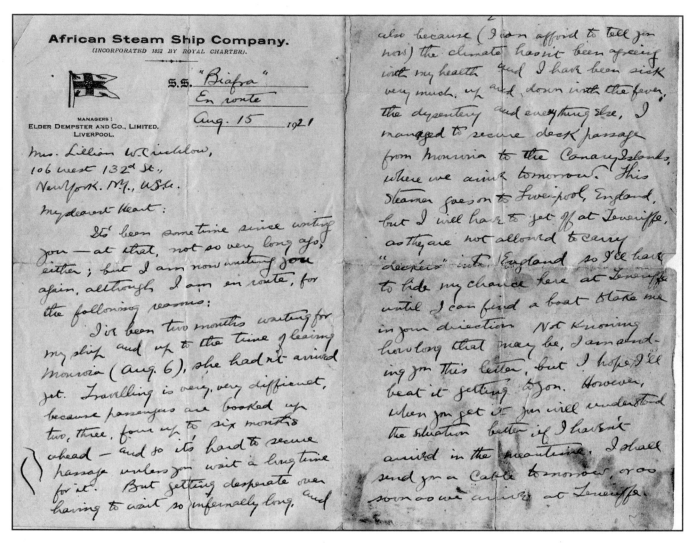

SS (Steamship) Biafra
En Route
August 15, 1921
Mrs. Lillian W. Crichlow
106 West 132nd Street
New York, New York USA

My dearest Heart:

It's been some time since writing you—at that, not so very long ago, either; but I am now writing you again, although I am en route, for the following reasons: I've been two months waiting for my ship and up to the time of leaving Monrovia (August 6), she hadn't arrived yet. Travelling is very, very difficult, because passengers are booked up two, three, four up to six months ahead—and so it's hard to secure passage unless you wait a long time for it. But getting desperate over having to wait so infernally long, and

page 2

also because (I can afford to tell you now) the climate hasn't been agreeing with my health and I have been sick very much, up and down with the fever, the dysentery and everything else. I managed to secure deck passage from Monrovia to the Canary Islands where we arrive tomorrow. This steamer goes on to Liverpool, England but I will have to get off at Teneriffe, as they are not allowed to carry "deckers" into England so I'll have to bide my chance here at Teneriffe until I can find a boat to take me In your direction. Not knowing how long that may be, I am sending you this letter but I hope I'll beat it getting to you. However, when you get it you will understand the situation better if I haven't arrived in the meantime. I shall send you a cable tomorrow or as soon as we arrive at Teneriffe.

-3-
Anyhow, you will have the consolation of knowing that I'm on my way.
I do not fear that I will be getting sick any more, altho Dr. Johnson says I ought to put myself under treatment some more after arriving New York and get the fever sweated out of me. I have been some sick, all right, but did not write you about it, so you do not worry unnecessarily. I had the terrible black-water fever, too, which is considered very, very dangerous. My water, perspiration, stool, would be black; but Dr. Johnson (the American Minister) and Laurence the Druggist pulled me through.
I have been having a wonderful fight along some lines

with Mayor Johnson (the Potentate) and Mr. Marke (the Supreme Deputy) which I will explain more when I arrive. They are both of them rascals, and wanted to lay plans to steal as much of the Association's money as they could—but, of course I got in the way, and stirred them up against me. They have got some funny practices in Liberia, so that it is very, very difficult to write the truth about the place and the people thru the mails, which account for my keeping quiet on lots of subjects and for writing very favorably on others. Diplomacy, that's all. They open one's mail, incoming or outgoing, to find out what's going on. But 'nuff sed! You can put things together for yourself.
Love for yourself and the boys—heaps and heaps and oodles and oodles of it; while I remain,
As ever, Affectionately & loyally,
"C"

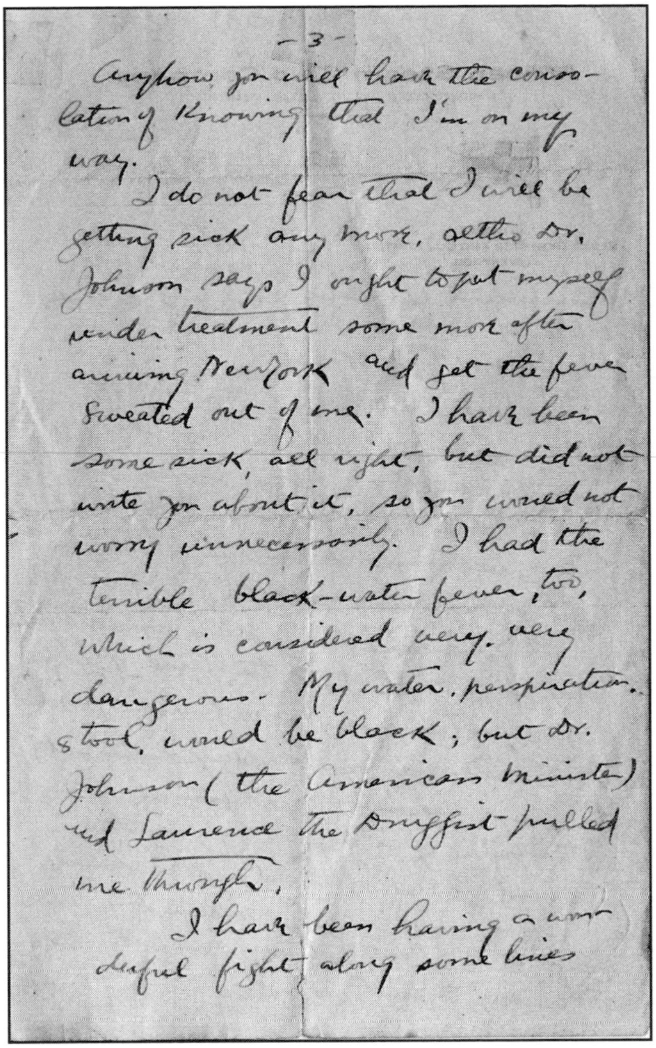

page 3
Anyhow, you will have the consolation of knowing that I'm on my way.

I do not fear that I will be getting sick any more, although Dr. Johnson says I ought to put myself under treatment some more after arriving New York and get the fever sweated out of me. I have been some sick, all right, but did not write you about it , so you would not worry unnecessarily. I had the terrible black-water fever, too, which is considered very, very dangerous. My water, perspiration, stool, would be black; but Dr. Johnson (the American Minister) and Laurence the Druggist pulled me through.

I have been having a wonderful fight along some lines

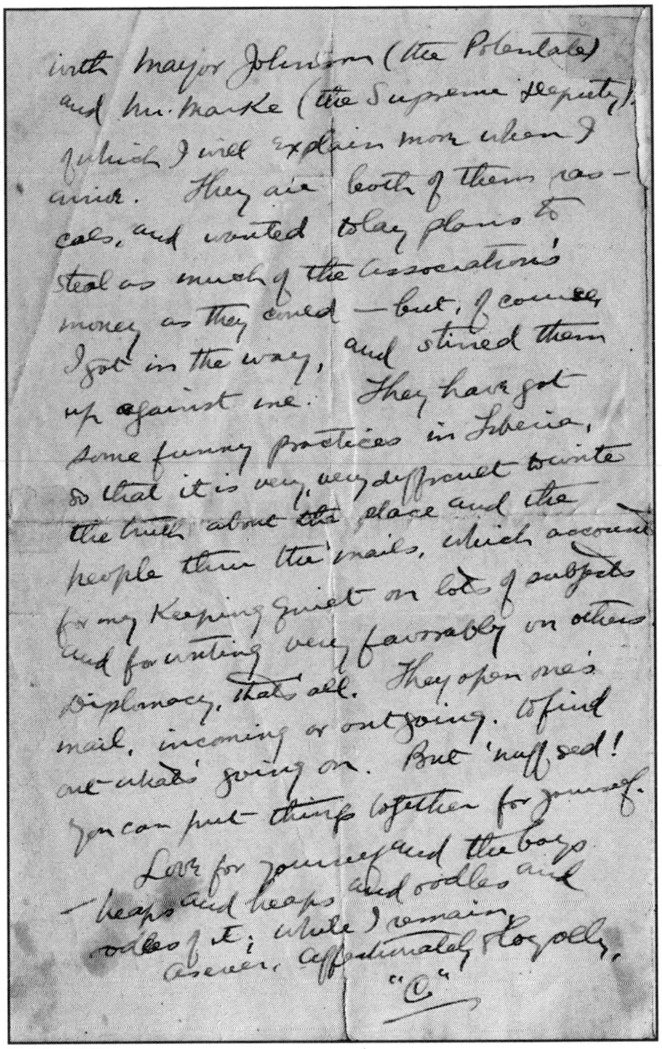

page 4
with Mayor Johnson (the Potentate) and Mr. Marke (the Supreme Deputy) of which I will explain more when I arrive. They are both of them rascals, and wanted to lay plans to deal as much of the Association's money as they could—but, of course I got in the way, and stirred them up against me. They have got some funny practices in Liberia, so that it is very, very difficult to write the truth about the place and the people thru the mails, which account for my keeping quiet on lots of subjects and for writing very favorably on others.

Diplomacy, that's all. They open one's mail, incoming or outgoing to find out what's going on. But 'nuff sed! You can put things together for yourself.

Love for yourself and the boys- heaps and heaps and oodles and oodles of it; while I remain

As ever, Affectionately loyally,
"C"

Cyril Crichlow on balcony of building in Monrovia, Liberia, 1921

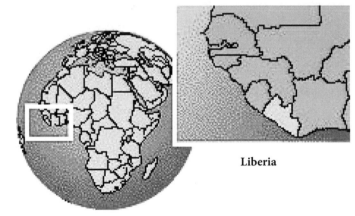

Liberia

Cyril's father, Samuel Crichlow, mother, Rebecca Pilgrim Crichlow. The other lady is probably one of Cyril's grandmothers.

Cyril and Lillian's three sons, Luther, Martin and Forrester, about 1920—the time that Cyril would have been traveling to Liberia.

CHAPTER 10:

LILLIAN ELIZABETH WARNICK CRICHLOW, MOTHER OF MARTIN A. CRICHLOW

Lillian Elizabeth Warnick was born in Salem, New Jersey, on October 31, 1889. She was the oldest child of Franklin George Warnick and Lucy Janet Miller Warnick. Lillian (Nana as she was called after her grandchildren were born), had eight sisters and brothers: Emily Naomi, Edith May, Paul Edward, William Hackett, Phillip, Rachel Olive, Andrew Matthew and Anna Maud.

Franklin Warnick was a minister in the Seventh Day Adventist Church in New Jersey. Lillian attended school in New Jersey. Her mother died in 1901 and for several years Lillian helped with the care of her siblings. When she was about 18 years old, she went to Alabama as a missionary of the Seventh Day Adventist Church. It was in Mobile, Alabama, that she married Cyril Askelon Crichlow, on May 30, 1909.

Lillian Warnick Crichlow

They both were involved in church missionary work. In 1910 they were living in Yazoo City, Mississippi where their first child, Luther Warnick Crichlow, was born on May 7, 1910. Their second child, Martin Augustus Crichlow, was born in Yazoo City in 1912. Their third son, Allwyn Forrester Crichlow, was born in Nashville, Tennessee, on January 11, 1915. Cyril and Lillian traveled quite a bit doing their mission work. They lived in several places in New York and also in several different cities in New Jersey.

It was about 1927 that Cyril came to Washington, and his middle son, Martin, came shortly after. About six months later, Lillian and their other two sons moved to Washington. They lived for a while at 716 23rd Street, NW. Cyril began a job at the Munitions Building as a messenger. Later he worked up to be supervisor of the Mail Room at the Navy Department of the U.S. government. Most women back there then did not work outside the home. Cyril's wife was a housewife and active member of the Seventh Day Baptist Church.

When I met Lillian Crichlow about 1939 she was living near Fourth and R Streets, NW, with two of the children, Martin and Forrester. She and Cyril Crichlow had divorced in 1933. Luther was at Alfred University, a Seventh Day Baptist school in New York, studying for the ministry after having earned a bachelor's degree from Howard University in 1935.

About the time that Martin and I married in November 1942, Lillian Crichlow (I called her Nana after my marriage) was nurse to a friend Mrs. Frances Carter at 7 N Street, SE, and lived there for a while.

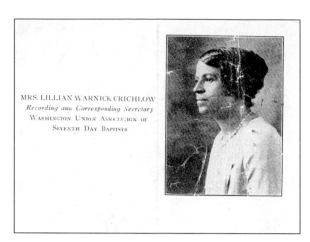

Lillian was raised as a Seventh Day Adventist but converted to Seventh Day Baptist after she married.

Nana had continued to study and earned her high school diploma from Cardozo's night school on June 21, 1939. On June 22, 1948, she received a diploma in practical nursing from the Margaret Murray Washington Vocational High School. (Margaret Mary Washington was the wife of the noted educator and practical arts/vocational education advocate Booker T. Washington.) After receiving her diploma Nana worked at Freedmen's Hospital as a nursing aide. She also worked as a nurse at Dr. Lillian Wheeler's office following those years. She had been a faithful member of the People's Seventh Day Baptist Church at 10th and V Streets, NW, where her oldest son, Luther, was pastor. Nana was pianist there; she probably had learned to play the piano while living in New Jersey and played quite well. In the late 1940s and early 1950s, Nana lived in Brandywine, Maryland, and took care of an elderly gentleman, Mr. Mahoney. Some say that the house they lived in had once been a school house.

When Forrester remarried about 1955, he and his second wife lived in that house with Nana. Forrester and Betty had 8 children: Bernard, Donna, Rachel, Martin, Gordon, Mary, Allen, and Betty, all of whom still live in the DC area. Nana helped Forrester and Betty with the children.

On the weekends, Nana often came into DC to attend church, and often stayed

Lillian Crichlow family portrait ca. 1905
Seated: Paul Warnick; Franklin Warnick (Lillian's father); Emma Taylor Warnick (Lillian's stepmother); William Warnick; Anna Maud Warnick, in father's lap; Andrew Warnick, in mother's lap. Standing rear: Lillian Warnick, Rachel Warnick, Naomi Warnick

100

with Mrs. Carter. She helped take care of a little girl named Candace and from time to time also stayed with her oldest granddaughter, Lillian Crichlow Burrell on Suitland Road, SE.

About 1960, Martin and some of his friends built another house (on the same site as the old schoolhouse) in Brandywine for Nana and the family lived there for several years until Forrester died in 1972. In the late 1970s, Nana moved to 1418 Longfellow Street, NW, a community group home for elderly people. Mrs. Hayes was the owner/operator.

The former Seventh Day Baptist Church that she had attended on 10th and V Streets had joined with the Washington Seventh Day Baptist Church at 16th and Crittenden Streets, NW, a mostly White group. They seemed very fond of her and would bring her to our house most Saturdays after service. I had retired in 1978 and during the week would sometimes drive her around to the clinic, and various places in the city where she wanted to go. I would visit her at least once a week and although she had lost her hearing completely by the time she reached 75 years of age, we would write messages to her. If I had kept them all, I would have several volumes, I suppose!

Nana's health remained fairly good. In the spring of 1984 she fell at the house where she was staying and her hip was broken. She was taken to the hospital for surgery and then transferred to the Wisconsin Nursing Home on Wisconsin Avenue, NW She died at the nursing home on October 5, 1984, at the age of 94 years, 11 months. If she had lived until October 31, she would have been 95 years old.

Her funeral arrangements were handled by Rhines Funeral Home. The funeral was held at the Washington Seventh Day Baptist Church, 4700 16th Street, NW, on Saturday, October 13,1984, at 2:00 p.m.. The members spoke very highly of her, including U. S. Senator Jennings Randolph, who was a member of the same church. Some told amusing stories about her. Her nieces, Bertha Sellers and Lillian Amos, came from Detroit and her brother, William, and his wife, Louise Warnick, came from Amissville, VA. I gave some remarks at the service and read a poem that I had written for her 90th birthday celebration that was held at our house. The Reverend Leland E. Davis, Pastor, officiated and gave the eulogy.

Nana's remains have been placed at the Rock Creek Cemetery, Rock Creek Church Road and Webster Street, NW, Section 5, Block 4, Lot 127. A headstone has been placed there along with some plants.

Linda: For a long time, some of us family members have been trying to determine when Lillian and Cyril became Seventh Day Baptists. In a July 3, 2012 email in response to a query from Linda, Nicholas J. Kersten, Librarian-Historian of the Seventh Day Baptist Historical Society replied:

> *I have attached a Sabbath Recorder article from October 8, 1923, which details the creation of a "Provisional Committee for work among the Colored People," at which time Cyril was asked to serve as field evangelist. At the time of the publication of this article, apparently enough money had been raised to pay his*

salary for a year. It notes that Cyril was a non-resident member of the Detroit SDB church. This is not surprising, as during this period the Detroit church and its pastor, Rev. Robert B. St. Clair, were ahead of its time in the promotion of civil rights. Likewise, St. Clair was in correspondence with several Black SDA churches in the Washington, D.C., area and elsewhere that had grown increasingly disillusioned with Seventh Day Adventists. In her obituary (also attached), it is said that she remembered becoming a Seventh Day Baptist, sight unseen, about 1925 after reading tracts put out by Rev. St. Clair. Between these two pieces of information, I think we can safely place their move to SDBs about 1923-1924.

As to the larger questions about SDBs and racial issues, I am proud to say that we were apparently, as a movement, somewhat ahead of the times. I'm certain that perhaps we were not always as benevolent as has sometimes been claimed by SDBs, but I am comfortable saying that at Alfred, at the time Luther was there, it wouldn't have been a significant issue. Alfred had allowed female students to sit alongside the male students at the advent of the suffrage movement (mid 1870s), and while Alfred wasn't a racially diverse community, I'm quite certain that it wouldn't have been an issue there of any consequence. SDBs were paying for the education of missionary children from around the world (China, Ghana, and elsewhere) by the 1920s. It might seem strange to think that a little group of people like SDBs were doing this kind of thing, but we have always been small, and that has worked to our advantage on matters of civil rights and racial and ethnic issues—if someone wants to associate with us, we have been glad to call them family. There are, for example, anecdotal stories which I believe, about SDB conference sessions being held in West Virginia in the early 1940s where SDBs refused to patronize businesses that they knew to be racist, on behalf of their non-White brothers and sisters.

Most of Nana's siblings and their families remained staunch Adventists and many were ministers, teachers, and missionaries. One of Nana's nieces, Lois Simons Benson, and her husband Dr. Lloyd Benson served as missionaries in Kenya in the 1950s. (See Minnie Simons' book about the Simons, A Colloquial History of A Black South Carolina Family Named Simons, *listed in For Further Reading).*

Recently I asked Lois how/why there seemed to have been a rift between Nana (Lillian) and her parents. Lois replied that not only did Nana reject the Adventist faith, she wrote letters to family members condemning it. Nana's father who was a Seventh Day Adventist minister wrote in a letter to another family member that he hoped Nana, along with sister Rachel and brother Rafael, would "return to the fold."

Nana stayed true to her SDB faith until the end and her son Luther became a Seventh Day Baptist minister.

Interestingly, later, after Lillian and Cyril divorced, Cyril seemed to have conducted his own "church" in his home. "Christian Discipleship of the World" was the name used on some of his publications.]

personality profile

LILLIAN CRICHLOW

We were in the midst of a church business meeting, engrossed in the tense task of "calling" a pastor. And the word of the Lord came to us--through Lillian Crichlow.

We had been working hard to make carefully calculated statements on all sides of the issue, managing neither to hide the emotion nor to reveal our thoughts. It seemed inappropriate to say things like, "What we really need is a black pastor to minister to this city." And certainly it would be unacceptable to say, "Can't you be a bit less of a snob when it comes to education and credentials?"

She stood up to speak. The metal chair clattered and someone grabbed for her cane while she tottered between her weak knee and her poor sense of balance. Her high-pitched, raspy voice jarred us out of our intense preoccupation with "our" problem.

I have no ideas what she said. There is no tape recording, no note taking, no remembering the factual details of such a meeting. I only know that as she talked, quoting Scripture and leading us in prayer as she often does, we became aware that our words were nothing. She is totally deaf. She had not heard any of them. Yet out of our midst she spoke as God to us-- accepting our emotion, knowing our thoughts, and pointing a clearer way than that we seemed prone to take.

In the months during which we lived with that day's decision (and others like it), it was often not the leaders we had chosen but the prophet God had raised up for us who spoke to our need. Hers is the message of all the prophets: God is concerned, God has a purpose, and God is participating in the events of His world.

Most people find Lillian Crichlow a more palatable prophet than Amos or Ezekiel. Her techniques are many. She can embarrass one into truth. In the midst of a worship service (forgetting that everyone is silent, because she can't hear silence any more than she can hear sound), she'll blurt out, "An educated person like you has no pen! How am I to hear the sermon if you don't write it for me?" And eventually she'll produce a blunt pencil stub and an almost-clean scrap of paper from her overstuffed handbag. (One discovers there is some message in every sermon!)

Or she can shame us into sensitivity. In the middle of a crowd she'll bop someone on the behind with a sharp crack of her cane and order him to "Do a little missionary work and help this old woman up the steps!"

She performs her more priestly duties with dignity and strength. Her tall black figure is usually clad in white when she serves Communion. Her voice carries the authority of

Gabriel's as she reads the Scripture to a Sabbath School class.

We remember the baptism service in which our small group filled only parts of the two front pews in a huge borrowed sanctuary (the closest available one with a baptistry). We felt rather lost in there even though we were adding our four more to the Kingdom. Then Mrs. Crichlow filled the whole huge space to the high arched dome reading the story of Jesus' baptism from Matthew. The voice from heaven echoed among us: "This is my beloved son in whom I am well pleased." (The deacon who stood near her later told us she had been holding her Bible open to Judges--upside down.)

Before she became deaf Mrs. Crichlow was a musician--organist, choir director, and teacher. Now, on those days that the choir seems to sound its worst, she'll rush up to the director after the service to say, "Oh, thank you, thank you! The choir sang just beautifully today!" Those nearby look stunned for a moment. Then they are suddenly also aware that the choir sang just beautifully today.

Prophets are never predictable. This one brought an antique figurine of a kitten to church one day and entrusted it to a busy young school-teacher mother who reluctantly agreed to repaint it for her. Every week Mrs. Crichlow would bug her about it. Was it done?

How was it going? The kitten survived a fight with a real cat and several re-touch-ups before it was finally delivered to Mrs. Crichlow, who promptly handed it back saying, "I had you do it for yourself!"

The prophetic vision is not a vision of the future. It is a glimpse of the mind of God. It is as she communicates her vision—her view of life—that Lillian Crichlow best exercises her gift of prophecy. At a recent church retreat she told this story of her mountaintop experience:

My father had just gone from Battle Creek, Michigan, down into the deep, dark South. Dad was a minister and times were kinda hard. We came into contact with a number of things that I'd never had any idea existed. He was to teach in an orphanage there in Chattanooga, Tennessee, and my mother was to be a matron.

Conditions there were not as my mother had expected them, and we had to find a different house. It was clear up on the top of a hill, ...and the thing that has impressed me all my life is that in spite of the hardships there I could get a view from the top of that hill where we lived away over to Lookout Mountain. I used to look over there as a child (I was the oldest of seven children) and I noticed one day there was a heavy, heavy cloud over atop of the mountain, but above this cloud the sun was shining.

As I looked closer I noticed birds flying around up there in the sun, and it was raining 'cause I could see the flashes of lightning and I knew that it was raining. And as I looked and saw those eagles flying above that dark, dark cloud in the sunshine, then and there I made up my mind that I too when I had trials in my life, when the dark days came, I was going to mount as the eagles did and rise above that cloud and bask in the sunshine of God's love.

I've had many occasions to remember that promise in my life. Many a time when the dark days came I had to go back to my childhood view of Lookout Mountain and mount as the eagles did above the dark clouds of life (as we all might have and will have), and I have been thankful for that lesson

I learned that no matter how dark the day, how cloudy, how much rain, still we can fly above it up in the sunshine of God's love. [1]

God knew this time how to get around the problem of a prophet not being accepted in his own country. Lillian Crichlow was born in Salem, New Jersey (1889), to a family who later made their home in twenty-eight different states from Yazoo, Mississippi, to Milton, Wisconsin, to Cambridge, Massachusetts. Her father began as a Baptist minister and later became a Seventh-day Adventist. [2]

Lillian married Cyril A. Crichlow, a native of Trinidad, who served as field secretary and evangelist for the Provisional Committee for Work Among Colored People, appointed in 1923 by the Eastern Association of Seventh Day Baptist Churches. Soon after that the Crichlows, both school teachers and accomplished musicians, became leaders of the People's Seventh Day Baptist Church in Washington, D.C.

Their oldest son, Luther W. Crichlow, graduated from Howard University and Alfred Theological Seminary, served as an Army chaplain in World War II, went with his wife as missionary to Jamaica for five years, and then was pastor of the People's Church (1946-58) until his death at age forty-eight. [3]

Later when Lillian's youngest son also died, leaving seven grandchildren and an emotionally ill wife, Lillian

would show a picture of the grandchildren then in her care and say, "I always wanted to be a missionary doctor in Africa. I've been a nurse and a midwife and a teacher, and now God has given me my own little Africa."

Her missionary concern reaches and involves the whole church family. Where was so and so today? Did someone call on him this week? Have you written to the Fullers in Africa this month? They need our prayers and support! The lists of her flock are endless.

Now that she communicates so much in writing, the scraps of left-over Sabbath Day conversation contain such gems as this account of her becoming a Seventh Day Baptist (over 50 years ago):

I never heard an SDB sermon nor attended such a service before I cast in my lot. It was through the reading of tracts and Elder St. Clair from Detroit, who visited us when I lived in Asbury Park, New Jersey. I joined the Detroit church about 1925 and have never regretted it... Eld. St. Clair's death was attributed to the Ku Klux Klan. [4]

(Rev. Robert B. St. Clair had organized the church in Detroit in 1921. He worked in publishing, Sabbath reform, promotion of mission work in Jamaica, Java, and South Africa, and as full-time employed chairman of the Vocational Committee of General Conference.

(continued on page 27)

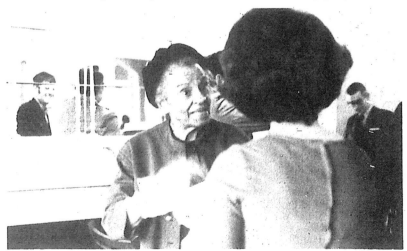

The prophetic vision is not a vision of the future..it is a glimpse of the mind of God. It is as she communicates her vision--her view of life--that Lillian Crichlow best exercises her gift of prophecy.

PERSONALITY PROFILE
(continued from page 9)

The denominational history notes that, "A great loss was sustained in his unexpected death in 1928.") [5]

In an article in the WASHINGTON SCENE in 1974 Mrs. Crichlow was quoted as saying that her main desire for the Washington Seventh Day Baptist Church (to which she transferred her membership in 1971) was to see it "progress through the increase of its membership." She indicated that when she entered the denomination, the denominational prayer seemed to be, "Lord, bless me and my wife, my son John and his wife, us four and no more." Thankfully she noted, we now appear to be rejecting this self-centered supplication for a more selfless one which "reaches out--and that's good!" [6]

In a recent Christmas letter to friends Mrs. Crichlow reminisced about Sabbath afternoons they had shared in Rock Creek Park: "How good it was to get out of the city there where it was quiet and we could relax. I live in such a tense world that I'm in need of relaxation quite a number of times. In fact every week I count the days from one Sabbath to another because I know I'm going to get out of my room and I can meet those of like precious faith."

After listing all the trips she made this past summer (to Association in Pennsylvania, to General Conference in Arkansas, to visit relatives in Virginia and in New Jersey, and to the church retreat in Maryland--all this at age eight-eight!), she ended the greeting on her usual tone of exhortation:

So I praise the Lord wonderfully even though I have the use of only one eye, can't hear a thing, and I got a bum knee; yet I know that my God cares for me (like all the rest of us). Let us keep trusting Him, put our trust in Him, that never failing trust, and we will be upheld in the everlasting arms!" [7] ☐

–Janet Thorngate

Editor's Note: The author, whose membership was in the Washington, D.C., church from 1971 to 1976, is now a member of the new church in Columbus, Ohio.

---

1 Transcript from a cassette tape recorded by Earl Hibbard in Washington, D.C., 1977.

2 From an article by Barbara Harrison (now Lacey) in THE WASHINGTON SCENE (newsletter of the Washington Seventh Day Baptist Church), January 1974.

3 *Seventh Day Baptists in Europe and America,* Vol. III, by Albert N. Rogers, Seventh Day Baptist Publishing House, 1972, pages 48, 52, 100, and 180.

4 Note written to Marie Bee in Washington, July 16, 1977.

5 *Seventh Day Baptists in Europe and America,* Vol. III, p. 42.

6 THE WASHINGTON SCENE, January 1974.

7 Letter to the Dale Thorngate family in Columbus, Ohio, December 1977.

†††
ACCESSIONS
†††

BAY AREA, CA
Theodore Hibbard, Pastor

By Testimony:
Iris Suhl

SECOND BROOKFIELD, N.Y.

By Baptism:
Robinette Balcom
Antoinette Balcom
Vicky Lynn Westcott
Emmie White

DALLAS—FT. WORTH, TX
Leo L. Floyd, Pastor

By Testimony:
Gregory Floyd
Thelma (Mrs. C.R.) Norton

By Letter:
Calvin P. Babcock
Meleta (Mrs. Calvin) Babcock

DENVER, CO
Edgar F. Wheeler, Pastor

By Letter:
Alice (Mrs. R. Michael) Parker
R. Michael Parker
Helen F. Wheeler

By Testimony:
Susan L. Stimson

NORTONVILLE, KS
Paul B. Osborn, Pastor

By Letter:
Mrs. Clifford (Carol) Bond
Clifford Bond

By Baptism:
Camille Bond

SALEM, W.V.
J. Paul Green, Pastor

By Testimony:
Barbara Seminick

WASHINGTON, D.C.
Leland E. Davis, Pastor

By Testimony:
Douglas Rausch

BOOK REVIEW

A fascinating new book, *African Fables* by Eudene Keidel, skillfully retells twenty-one animal stories with a spiritual truth as used by Christian preachers and teachers in Zaire.

These fables, with their insight into human nature and foibles, have been passed from generation to generation in Africa from time immemorial.

"During our four terms of missionary service in Zaire, I have often heard Africans tell stories drawn from their folklore," the author comments.

"I've heard pastors use them from the pulpit to teach spiritual lessons. I've listened to older village people relate them around the fire at night. I've read some from their literature," she continues.

"I've told these stories to children in many places and now share some of them with you."

African Fables, by Eudene Keidel, features the adventures and amusing antics of turtles, parrots, leopards, crows, lizards, snails, monkeys, lions, rats, frogs, sparrows, crocodiles, foxes, elephants, moles, canaries, goats, pigs, and other animals-including a memorable account of an encounter between a fly and a hippopotamus.

The stories encourage friendship and goodwill, equality and cooperation, trustworthiness, respect for parents, loyalty, and other Christian character traits.

The animals and people in *African Fables* resolve their conflicts and untangle themselves from their dilemmas with startling cleverness. Those who read or hear these accounts will not soon forget the lessons taught in this unique way.

The fables "are also adaptable for sermon material and public speakers' illustrations," Edwin J. Statler points out in *Provident Bookfinder.* "The book would make a fine gift."

African Fables, by Eudene Keidel, published by Herald Press, Scottdale, Pennsylvania, and Kitchener, Ontario, is available in bookstores in a quality softcover edition at $1.95. ☐

CHAPTER 11

MARTIN'S BROTHERS

Luther Warnick Crichlow

LUTHER WARNICK CRICHLOW

Luther was born in Yazoo City, Mississippi. He graduated from Dunbar High School in 1930 and earned his B.A. degree at Howard University in 1935 and his bachelor of divinity degree at The Seventh Day Baptist school, Alfred University, New York, in 1938. He played trumpet at both schools and earned letters for his band excellence.

He married Martha Archer in November 1938. They had no children.

During World War II he served as an Army chaplain overseas and was a chaplain in the Army Reserve until his death in 1958. He served as pastor of People's Seventh Day Baptist Church. Just after his marriage in 1938, he and Martha sailed to Jamaica where he served as a Seventh Day Baptist missionary. According to some sources Luther also worked in the Federal government as a mail clerk, in the same division his father, Cyril, had worked.

Crichlow family at Arlington Cemetery following Luther's funeral. Left to right, standing: Forrester; Cyril; Unknown; William Warnick (Uncle Bill); Lillian Warnick Crichlow; Bill's wife, Louise Warnick; Martin; Martha; Allwyn Forrester Jr., Lillian; Forrester's wife, Betty Crichlow. Front: Donald Simons and Linda.

same church, he was ordained to the ministry on October 9, 1938, by a Seventh Day Baptist Council, which included Dean Bond. It was in this church that he was united in holy matrimony to Martha Archer on November 3, 1938. They sailed together to the British West Indies on the ninth, where they served as missionaries in charge of the Seventh Day Baptist work for more than five years.

Luther began to work on the Jamaica School fund and rejoiced over the first shilling collected by the Jamaican brethren toward the present work which is now fully established there. He believed in and advocated self-reliance. His motto was: "God helps those who help themselves."

He was a lover of music and presented for the first time in Jamaica "The Seven Last Words" by DuBois. He had played in the Howard University band and the U. S. Department of Agriculture orchestra.

He possessed unusual literary ability and at one time served as editor of the Young People's Page in the Sabbath Recorder.

During World War II, he was an Army chaplain at Calendonia, New Hebrides, Guadalcanal, Luzon, and Ascam City, Korea, serving with the Armed Forces Service Units. At the time of his death, he was also serving as chaplain of the 317th Infantry Regiment, U. S. Army Reserves.

He was installed as pastor of the People's Seventh Day Baptist Church, 10th and V Streets, N. W., Washington, D. C., in 1946, and labored faithfully and diligently in this post, giving of his time and talents, conscientiously and unselfishly, in spite of many difficulties and trying problems, and serving there until the time of his last illness.

On Wednesday, July 2, 1958, his body lay in state at the People's Seventh Day Baptist Church and on Thursday, July 3, the funeral services were held at the Metropolitan A. M. E. Church, because it afforded greater seating capacity. The host pastor, the Rev. G. Dewey Robinson, gave the Call to Worship and the following ministers assisted in the services, either by active participation or their presence: Elder J. Arthur Frey, acting pastor of the Seventh Day Baptist Church; Rev. Eliza-

beth F. Randolph, Seventh Day Baptist minister; Elder Donald Simons (Penna.), Adventist minister (cousin of the deceased); Father Benedict, Saint Barnabas Church, Brooklyn, N. Y. (another relative); Rev. Mr. Simms (Md.); Rev. Rebecca Glover, assistant pastor of Metropolitan A. M. E. Church; and Chaplain James T. Bard, of the United States Army Reserve, who delivered the eulogy. Chaplain Bard paid high tribute to Luther's service as a chaplain and told of his close experiences with men of all classes, creeds, races, and color. He said that in dealing with these men Luther always exhibited a fine Christian spirit in his every word, action, and deed.

He further stated that Luther felt that no man was inferior to him and that no man was his superior. The presence of persons of many races, creeds, color, and those representing various stations in life reflected his beliefs and practices.

Luther's three favorite hymns were sung during the course of the services: "I Am Thine, O Lord," "The Old Rugged Cross," and "The Lord's Prayer." He was buried at the Arlington National Cemetery with full military honors.

He was a faithful and devoted husband and son, a consecrated child of God, and a loyal and hard-working pastor of his flock. Besides his wife, Martha, a District of Columbia public school teacher, he leaves to mourn his loss his father, Cyril; his mother, Lillian; two brothers, Martin and Allwyn; four nieces, two nephews, and a host of other relatives and friends.

"O what their joy, and the glory must be, Those endless Sabbaths those blessed ones see; Crown for the valiant; for weary ones rest; God shall be all, and in all, ever blest."

"Father, in Thy gracious keeping, leave we now Thy servant sleeping."

— Martha A. Crichlow.

It is related of the great Scotch surgeon, Sir James Simpson, that he was once approached by a young man who wished to compliment him by asking what he regarded his greatest discovery, and the simple reply of this eminent scientist was, "My greatest discovery is that I am a great sinner and that Jesus is a great Savior."

Reverend Luther W. Crichlow

Born in Yazoo City, Mississippi, May 7, 1910;
Graduate of Howard University, 1935, A.B. Degree;
Graduate of School of Theology (Seventh Day Bapt'st), Alfred University, 1938, B.D. Degree; Missionary in charge of Seventh Day Baptist Mission Work in Jamaica, British West Indies, November, 1938, to December, 1943; Chaplain in the United States Army from February, 1944, to June, 1946 with Twenty-three Months Overseas Service in the Pacific Theater; Elected Pastor of the People's Seventh Day Baptist Church June 1, 1946.

Installation Services

of

Reverend Luther W. Crichlow

as PASTOR of

The People's Seventh Day Baptist Church

Tenth and V Streets, Northwest

Washington, D. C.

July 15 - 22, 1946

Order of Installation Services

† † †

SUNDAY, JULY 21, 1946 — 3:30 O'CLOCK P. M.

Master of Ceremonies—Brother Leo Oxley

Prelude	Mrs. Lillian W. Crichlow
Invocation	Brother Leo Oxley
The Lord's Prayer	The Congregation
The Doxology	The Congregation
Scripture	Rev. Lester G. Osborn

Pastor, Seventh Day Baptist Church, Shiloh, N. J.

Prayer	Reverend W. M. Rustin
Hymn	"Majestic Sweetness Sits Enthroned"
Installation Sermon	Dean Ahva J. C. Bond

Dean, School of Theology (Seventh Day Baptist),
Alfred University, Alfred, New York

Vocal Solo	Mrs. Ruth Larkins

Accompanied by Miss Sylvia Larkins

Charge to the Pastor	Reverend Jerry A. Moore, Jr.

Pastor, Nineteenth Street Baptist Church

Hymn	"A Charge to Keep I Have"
Charge to the Church	Reverend Harold E. Snide

Pastor, Evangelical Seventh Day Baptist Church
Washington, D. C.

Vocal Solo	Mrs. Ella Bryan
Offering—	
Greetings	Reverend D. F. Johnson

Chaplain (Major) U. S. Army Reserve Corps

Presentation of Reverend Luther W. Crichlow, Pastor,
People's Seventh Day Baptist Church

Prayer	Reverend D. F. Johnson
Vocal Solo	Miss Lillian Giles
Greetings	Colonel West A. Hamilton

Office of the Secretary of War

Hymn	"All Hail the Power of Jesus' Name"
Benediction	

MISS ARCHER WAS RADIANT

These are the participants in the wedding of Miss Martha Clementine Archer, daughter of Aaron T. Archer, to the Rev. Luther Warnick Crichlow, son of Mr. and Mrs. Cyril A. Crichlow, which was solemnized Thursday. From left to right are: Lemuel Horne, Miss Louise Burwell, Martin Crichlow, Mr. and Mrs. Luther Crichlow, the bride and bridegroom, Miss Crozet Woods, Lawrence Hill, Miss Louise Lee, and James Mitchell. The ring-bearer is Master Clarence Gardner, and the flower girl is Patricia E. Wilson.—Photo by Scurlock.

Archer-Crichlow Wedding Is Brilliant Affair

In the flower-decked setting of Peoples Seventh Day Baptist Church, Miss Martha Clementine Archer, daughter of Aaron Thomas Archer, became the bride of Luther Warnick Crichlow, son of Mr. and Mrs. Cyril A. Crichlow, Thursday. The Rev. Frank Peterson officiated.

The bride is a recent graduate of Howard University and the bridegroom received his degree at Howard in 1935, and his doctor of divinity degree at Alfred University this year.

The bride, who was given away by her father, wore a white lace redingote over soft georgette crepe. A long tulle veil floated out from a coronet around her hair. She carried a bouquet of white roses and tiny white chrysanthemums.

Charming Bridesmaids

The bridesmaids were Leticia Owens, Louise Burwell, Crozet Woods, and Louise Lee. They wore dresses of blue lace and small coronets made of the same material, and bouquets of pink rosebuds.

The bridegroom was attended by his brother, Martin A. Crichlow and the ushers were Lemuel Horne, Lawrence Hill, and James Mitchell.

The flower girl, Patricia E. Wilson, made a charming picture as she took care of her floral duties. The ring-bearer was Clarence Gardner.

The reception followed immediately after at the home of the bride where the many beautiful gifts were on display. Soon after the couple left for Rhode Island where the Rev. Mr. Crichlow will meet with the mission board before leaving for New York. From there the two will sail for Kingston Jamaica, B.W.I., where he will take charge of the mission work of the Seventh Day Baptist Church.

Among the guests were:

Mrs. R. B. Shepard and Mrs. E. Barns, Miss Gorgetta White, Mrs. Madeline Kirkland, A. Forrester Crichlow, the Rev. Raymond Hunter;

The Rev. Sandy Parks, the Rev. Frank L. Peterson and daughter, Miss Pauline Groome, Mrs. William Beaman, Mrs. Prince Beaman;

Mr. and Mrs. Theodore Anderson, Mrs. Louis Sewell, Mrs. G. L. Golton, Mr. and Mrs. H. Harrington, Mr. and Mrs. R. C. Archer, Mrs. Bessie Carter;

Mrs. Annie Sampson, Mrs. Mary Gregba, Mrs. Clarence E. Garner, Mrs. Swann and daughter Mr. and Mrs. Chester E. Walker;

Mr. and Mrs. Oliver Holmes, Mrs. Huffman and daughter, Mr. and Mrs. Ed. Bredden, Mr. and Mrs. M. McIntree, Miss Pearl Franklin;

Miss Gertrude Brown, Miss Hattie Walton, Miss Maretta Stevens, Miss Martha McCord, Eugene Ford, and Marcus Hill.

The Baltimore Afro-American, Nov 12, 1938, p. 8.

ALLWYN FORRESTER CRICHLOW

Forrester ca. 1965

Born in Nashville, Tennessee, in 1916, Forrester attended grammar school in Asbury Park, New Jersey. After moving to Washington about 1928, he attended the renowned Dunbar High School.

Forrester married Irene Hemsley about 1937 and had two lovely children, Allwyn Forrester, Jr., and Lillian. They divorced about 1948.

Later Forrester married Betty Mason and together they had 8 children. All 10 of Forrester's children still live in the Washington, DC, area and are living successful, productive lives!

Forrester worked as a machinist at the Naval Ordinance Station in Indian Head, Maryland. He died of complications from diabetes in 1972.

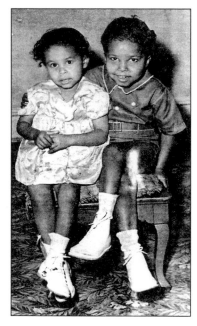

Lillian and Allwyn Crichlow, Forrester's children with his first wife Irene Hemsley Crichlow ca. 1945.

**Standing Allen, Mary, Rachel, Betty Crichlow-Eberhardt
Sitting: Bernard, Gordon, Donna, Martin, ca. 2005**

Nana's oldest grandchildren, Lillian Crichlow Burrell and Allwyn Crichlow, with Martin, Marietta, and Senator Jennings Randolph following Nana's memorial service in 1984.

Forrester ca. 1942

Forrester's wife Betty, their children, spouses, and Forrester and Betty's grandchildren.
Bottom left to right: Monica, Ericka, Terance, Raphael, Adrienne, Martin Luther
Middle: Mother-Betty, Mary, Rachel, Martin's wife Nellie, Marietta, Betty
Standing: Tim Eberhardt, Ben Canah, Allen Crichlow
Picture taken in September 1992 at Eric and Linda's house following Martin's memorial service.

Nana and Forrester at People's SDB
church, 1959.

Nana with her brother Uncle Bill—
Rev. William Warnick.

Marietta, Nana, Irene (Forrester's
first wife) with Lillian (daughter of
Forrester and Irene) in foreground.

CHAPTER 12

OUR DAUGHTER
LINDA MARIE CRICHLOW

Linda's 6 mo old picture

Linda was born on Thursday, August 4, 1949, at Freedmen's Hospital, 6th and Bryant Streets, NW, Washington, DC, at 1:34 AM. That was an exciting day for us. We stayed at Freedmen's Hospital for two days before coming home. Back there then, most new mothers and their babies stayed at the hospital for at least a week, sometimes longer. But the nurse said that some babies had been ill so they sent the well ones home as soon as possible. Martin, Edna, Linda, and I lived at 2024 Fourth Street, NW, not far from the hospital.

Linda was a healthy baby. I stayed home from work until the first day of February then my friend, Hattie Beasley, who lived on Second Street, NW, took care of her during the day. Martin's co-worker, who drove him to work at the Pentagon, would pick up Linda and Martin, drop her off at Hattie's house, then he and Martin would go on to work. Linda seemed to enjoy the company of Hattie's little boy, William (Pudney) Beasley who was born on March 19, 1949.

While I was on maternity leave with Linda, Martin and I looked for a different place to live. On January 30, 1950, we moved from 2024 Fourth Street to 543 Randolph Street NW, and it is in this residence that I have lived ever since.

When we moved to Randolph Street, Edna came with us. The Fourth Street house

Children in front of Mt. Carmel, ca. 1956.
Left to right: Linda, Vashon Jackson, Krishana Cash, Velma Jackson. Vashon and Velma were children of Almarion Stoakley Jackson, Marietta's childhood friend.

112

543 Randolph Street house

Linda's 3rd birthday party with neighbor children

was sold, later repurchased, then rented out. The people who purchased 2024 4th Street had not been able to keep up the payments. Edna tells how she later stood on the sidewalk outside the house to buy the house back when it was auctioned.

Edna was very helpful when our daughter Linda was born. She and a friend sewed and made a bassinet cover, a dress, a little embroidered jacket, and cap. She was helpful in sitting with Linda when I attended night classes and had to go out.

When Linda was two years old, we sent her to the Tiny Tots Nursery School located on Irving Street, NW, near Warder, not far from our house on Randolph Street, NW. A lady named Buena Vista Banks was director of the nursery school.

Martin would drive us to Mount Carmel Baptist Church at Third and I Streets, NW, and Linda was enrolled in the nursery class there. She and I also became members of the Madrecias (Mother Daughter, in Spanish) Club when she was two years old. My friend Phyllis Fauntleroy had invited us to join. She had organized the club with her two little girls, Phylicia and Jacqueline, along with some others. The limit on the membership of the mothers was twelve.

It was a nice group and held monthly meetings for the mothers and monthly activities for the children. Social activities were held from time to time and fathers were invited.

When the children graduated from high school their meetings were stopped but the club has had reunions from time to time. The Madrecia daughters have all gone to college. Some have MD and Ph.D. degrees.

We were fortunate to have some lovely neighbors on Randolph Street. Mr. and Mrs. Alex Ferrara lived next door at 541. They had two children in elementary school. Janeth, the younger daughter was about 6 years old when we moved to Randolph Street and her sister Rita was about 8 years old. The schools in Wash-

Linda: with all the changes brought on by the 1954 school desegregation, the schools probably had a hard time figuring out which schools to include in which boundary. In many neighborhoods, there was a school on almost every other block. There had to be a school for Blacks and a school for Whites! As late as the early 2000s the school system was still dealing with the surplus of school buildings part of which was caused by duplicate buildings for the different races.

113

Sewing machine Aunt Edna gave Linda

ington were not desegregated until 1954 but Mrs. Ferrara (Bamah) would take Linda to programs that her daughters participated in at the then all-White Petworth Elementary School. No one ever had better neighbors than the Ferraras. As the children grew older, Rita and Janeth would babysit with Linda or would come over and play with her. The family moved to Wheaton when Linda was about six years old. We visited them there and they would visit us.

As I write this in November of 2001, Mr. and Mrs. Ferrara and Janeth have passed on. Rita and her grown son came to visit me recently. He is a college student.

In September of 1954, Linda started public school at Petworth Elementary. That was the year that the Supreme Court declared separate schools based on race as unconstitutional.

Colored children were then allowed to attend the formerly "White" schools. I was still recovering from the stillborn birth on August 15, so Martin took Linda to start kindergarten. He said that one of the little White boys looked at Linda and said, "I am White and you are Colored. Linda looked up at Martin and said, "I'm not Colored, am I, Daddy?" She had never heard people described like that before.

Linda did well at Petworth. She attended Petworth in Kindergarten and 1st grade, when the boundary line was changed and she had to attend Park View Elementary school for 2nd grade. Park View was a few blocks from us at Warder and Newton Streets. The boundary line was changed again at the end of her 2nd grade year so she returned to Petworth which was closer to us anyway. (See the book *First Class*, listed in For Further Reading, for more information about boundary changes in Washington, DC)

At the end of 5th grade, her 1st grade teacher Mrs. Hardy called me to say that Linda should be transferred to an honors program at Park View that Petworth did not have. So, for part of 6th grade she attended the honors class at Parkview. The program was just getting underway and actually did not seem to be as far advanced as Linda's classes at Petworth were. So Linda was transferred back to Petworth where she finished the sixth grade in June of 1960. She was the valedictory speaker and received a valedictory pin.

While she was at Petworth, the teachers had some excellent programs for the children. Linda's fourth grade teacher, Miss Heyman, was one special teacher. She taught them Russian Cossack dancing and other international folk dancing which they performed for one of the DC Teacher's Association meetings. She took them on field trips and made learning interesting for her pupils.

Linda attended the MacFarland Junior High School at 13th Street and Iowa Ave., NW. During the summer she did volunteer work with the American Red Cross. The years passed swiftly and it did not seem long before she had graduated and moved on to Roosevelt Senior High School at 13th and Upshur Streets, NW. She participated in various activities there and received a certificate for her membership and participation in the National Thespian Society. Mr. Alston W. Burleigh

114

was the teacher in charge of the group. They performed very well.

Linda excelled in clothing (sewing) in her home economics classes. She received a sterling silver place setting along with her award from the DC Department of Home Economics.

Robert Boyd, one of our friends, was principal of Roosevelt at that time. Mrs. Floretta McKenzie had been social studies teacher there and later became a counselor. When Linda became a senior, Mrs. McKenzie was her counselor. Mrs. McKenzie went on to earn her Ph.D and became superintendent of the public schools in the District of Columbia. She had an aunt who lived second door from me. Dr. McKenzie is now head of her own educational consulting group. (She also became chairwoman of the Howard University Board of Trustees and served the community in many other capacities) Linda graduated from Roosevelt Senior High School in June 1967.

During the summer of 1967 she worked as a teacher's aide with the Head Start Program at Park View Elementary school. In 1969 she worked as maintenance and sanitation Supervisor at a cafeteria with the General Services Administration. During the summer of 1970 she was a clerk typist with the General Services Administration.

Edna gave Linda a little sewing machine when she was about eight years old. Linda loved it. Sewing became her hobby. I never taught her to sew. She studied sewing in both junior and senior high school. She just seemed to have a talent for it. While she was in high school, she sewed and mended things for some of the teachers. She made dresses and other things for me and for herself. We have an album that has the first doll dress she made and pictures of the outfits she made while she was attending high school. Lots of nights she would be up late sewing. Some of her classmates would bring their school sewing projects to her for help. She has made suits, coats and lots of things for me, for herself, and for others.

By the time Linda was ready for college, the "White" colleges had become a bit more liberal and were accepting Colored students. When I was a college student, very few "White" colleges in the DC area admitted Colored students. It was about 1948 that the White colleges began to permit Colored students to enroll. Linda had applied to the University of Cincinnati and was accepted there. We had gone with her during the spring to look the college over. I remember it was there in 1967 that I saw a microwave oven for the first time! Linda had applied to major in home economics and one of the teachers demonstrated how a glass of water could be heated in the microwave. They had just come on the market. Now, almost every kitchen has one.

Linda attended the University of Cincinnati in Ohio during the time when many young people were participating in the Civil Rights Movement. She was very active in the Black Student Union on campus and other organizations. One of her good friends there was Paulette Fears, a cousin of Elizabeth Campbell, one of Martin's classmates at Hampton. Another was Linda Walton, a cousin of my

Faustine Childress Jones-Wilson says that 90% of Black students attended HBCU's in 1941 but it must be noted that there were Blacks at the "White schools even in the 1800s. WEB Du Bois and Carter G. Woodson, founder of Negro History Week were both Harvard class of 1912. Many Blacks attended Oberlin in the mid-1800s, including ancestors of our friends the Fauntleroys. Ida Gibbs Hunt, Cousin Ida to all, was Oberlin class of 1884.

Bowdoin College and Williams College in Maine and the University of Chicago were among other schools who admitted African Americans early on. I didn't learn until 2006 that we had a cousin, Charles Bruce—Aunt Goldie's son—who was Harvard class of 1933, along with Dr. Frank Snowden who was Academic Dean of Howard U from 1956-1968.

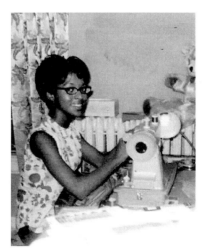

Linda at her sewing machine 1967

115

YELLOW JACKET

— A Living Laboratory in Human Relations —

Volume 2, Number 9   West Virginia State College, Institute, West Virginia   April 1, 1971

Home Ec Major Plans Summer Trip to Africa

Linda Crichlow, a Home Economics major here at State is planning a trip to Africa this summer. Linda will be West Virginia State's official representative in the Operation Crossroads Africa Program. Crossroads exists primarily as a vehicle of communication. Its basic aim is to create a structure in which North Americans and Africans can develop some understanding of each other's point of view.

Several groups of people go each summer. The group is the primary unit in the Crossroads program. It consists of approximately ten college-age students and a leader, and is assembled to assure as wide a cross-section of individuals as possible in terms of race, social and regional backgrounds, and religion.

Linda wants to go because she thinks it would be an invaluable experience. She feels that traveling and meeting new people is as important a part of her education as are any of the required courses.

"Good communication is the key to all human growth and development. Everybody's talking about "involvement" today. Participating in Crossroads is one way I can get involved."

As a representative for Crossroads, Linda must raise $1500. Raising at least part of the cost of going is proof of the Crossroaders commitment to the program.

Private donations are welcomed. Make checks payable to Operation Crossroads Africa, Inc. and send them to Dr. Naomi Garrett in the Modern Language Department. The donations are tax exempt.

Crossroads Africa

By Linda Crichlow

Thanks for making it possible for me to spend my summer in Africa. It proved to be one of the best experiences I've ever had. Through your contributions of time, money and encouragement, I was able to participate in Operation Crossroads Africa.

Crossroads sent approximately 150 students to West Africa this year, with groups in Nigeria, Liberia, Ivory Coast, Ghana and the Camerouns. My group consisted of 11 Americans, two Ghanaians and two Ivorians. We lived in Anfoeta, a tiny village in the Volta Region of Ghana, and built a four-room schoolhouse of cinderblocks. We completed everything except the roof because the village ran out of money and materials, but they promised us the school would be completed by this fall's school term.

Our group lived a very rural life with no plumbing or electricity. However, it was lots of fun going to the nearby stream to get water and going across the road to the toilets. We even survived the mosquitos, sandflies, and other insects. On the weekends we often visited Accra, the capital of Ghana, which is not unlike any large American city. We also visited the capitals of three other countries, Togo, Dahomey and the Ivory Coast.

If anyone is interested in hearing more about my experiences, contact me personally or contact Dr. Naomi Garrett, chairman of the Crossroads committee. I would be delighted to show my slides to any individuals, classes or clubs and tell you about my trip.

These are members of the group Linda lived with in Ghana during the summer of 1971.
That experience changed her life. Later, she and others founded the Operation Crossroads Africa DC Alumni.

friend Hattie Walton Beasley. Linda stayed at the University of Cincinnati for two years before transferring to West Virginia State College in Institute, West Virginia, not far from Charleston. While majoring in home economics at West Virginia State College, Linda participated in many activities. She continued to sew and make friends. I remember that she told me that she made cummerbunds for all the members of the Omega fraternity there.

During the summer of 1971, she went to West Africa as a representative from West Virginia State College with the Operation Crossroads Africa program, an organization based in New York City designed to improve relations between Africans and Americans by visiting each others' countries and exchanging ideas and knowledge of each others' lifestyles. She lived for six weeks in the village of Anfoeta, Ghana, and spent two additional weeks traveling in the neighboring countries of Togo, Dahomey (which is now called the Republic of Benin), and the Ivory Coast, in addition to visiting other towns and cities of Ghana. There were several White college students participating in this activity. Some came with Linda to visit us in Washington.

Linda seemed to like Africa and the people there liked her. One African couple in Anfoeta named their daughter "Linda Marie." In the summer of 1973, Linda returned to Africa, traveling alone as a tourist. She visited friends in parts of East Africa including Tanzania, Kenya, Ethiopia, the Sudan and also, England. Linda made many life-long friends during her Crossroads experience and later was one of the founding members of the Operation Crossroads Africa DC Alumni organization which consisted of folks who had traveled to Africa with Crossroads.

When Linda was a senior at West Virginia State College, she had the opportunity to do her practice teaching in Brooklyn, New York, District 13, which bordered Fort Greene and Bedford Stuyvesant. There, the students were predominantly

117

Eric and Linda's wedding, November 27, 1976.
l-r, Rev. Moses Beasley, Sheila Ross Smith, matron of honor, Martin, Marietta, Linda, Eric, Irene, Mark, Stanley White, best man. Rev. Beasley officiated at Martin and Marietta's wedding and at Linda's, Kwame's and Khalila's christenings. Stanley (Ayo now) Eric's first cousin, later changed his name to Ayokunle Odeleye.

Puerto Rican and Black but the staff was mostly White (many Jewish). Some local leaders, including future New York State Assemblyman Al Vann and JHS 117 principal Alton Rison wrote a proposal to recruit students from historically Black colleges and universities (HBCUs) in the hope that some would stay and teach in District 13. Linda took advantage of this.

In May 1972 Linda received her bachelors degree in home economics from West Virginia State College and also an honorary award from Who's Who among Students in American Universities and Colleges. In the fall of 1972 she began her teaching career at Junior High School No. 117. She taught foods and nutrition there and taught dressmaking during the evening at the East New York Youth and Adult Center in Brooklyn.

In 1974, Linda taught an in-service human relations course during the fall term in New York. In the class were forty other teachers from various schools in Brooklyn school District 13. She coordinated activities and discussions related to the Board of Education's television program "Breaking the Barriers," a program concerned with human relations in the schools.

After the end of the 1974-75 school term in New York, Linda returned to Washington. She taught foods and nutrition during the day and sewing classes to adults in the evening at Woodson High School and soon began her studies toward a master's degree in human ecology at Howard University. While earning her MS degree she worked as a graduate assistant in the school of human ecology and also as a research aide. She received her master's degree in May 1979 in microenvironmental studies and design. Her thesis was entitled *Traditional Textiles and Clothing of Nepal.*

Shortly after Linda returned from New York, some of the friends she had met there came to visit. One day one of the New York teachers, her first name was Helen, was to come for lunch with a couple of other people Linda had met in New York. One young man arrived first and Linda and I met him at the door. I asked, "Is this Helen's friend?" Linda said, "Oh no, he is a friend of all of us." She introduced him to me. His name was Eric White. He had recently received his master's degree from Columbia University in New York and was in DC staying with his cousin, Stanley White (Ayokunle), a well-known artist. Linda and Eric had met at a gasoline station in New York when both were filling their cars at the pump. Soon after coming to Washington, Eric started to work as a reference librarian at Founders Library at Howard University.

In the fall of 1976 Linda and Eric began to plan their wedding. I tried to persuade them to have the wedding at the Howard University Chapel. But they wanted a home wedding. So, on November 27, 1976, they were married at 543 Randolph Street, NW. Reverend Moses Beasley performed the ceremony. Linda's good friend, Sheila Ross Smith, was her bridesmaid. Stanley White, Eric's cousin, was his best man. A beautiful reception was held at the Foxtrappe Club, 1601 R Street, NW. They lived at 744 Girard Street, NW, and in an apartment in Adelphi, Maryland, until 1980 when they purchased a house on Madison Street, NW. In 1992, they moved to Nicholson Street, NW, where they still reside.

Linda and Eric have been active in too many activities to mention here. They traveled to Nepal in the summer of 1979 and also to India, Egypt, and some countries in Europe. They have traveled to many places in the United States, attending various conventions and visiting friends and relatives. Linda went to Africa during the summer of 2000 as a delegate of the Home Economics Association to attend the International Federation Home Economics Conference in Accra, Ghana.

While she was there, she visited Anfoeta, where she had been a Crossroads Representative in 1971. Some of the villagers remembered her and gave a celebration in her honor. Linda is a member of several professional and civic organizations such as the American Home Economics Association, the DC Home Economics Association, Tots and Teens, and the American Library Association.

Their son, Kwame, was born in 1982. In 1984, their daughter, Khalila, was born. We were all excited and delighted. We are proud of both of them.

Linda worked from 1980 to 1984 as the Washington representative for Crossroads Africa and then taught briefly at Roosevelt High School from January to June 1986. She began teaching at Eastern High School in the Fall of 1986 and taught foods and nutrition there until 2004. She also taught occasional etiquette classes for children at the very nice restaurant, Blair Mansion Inn, at 7711 Eastern Avenue for several years.

Nicholson Street

Eric, Linda, Kwame, Khalila ca. 1985

Linda talking to Ghanaian Ambassador Quaison-Sackey during a Crossroads fundraiser at his residence (1979)

A highlight of Linda's teaching career was in 1992 when noted chef Julia Child spent a day in her classroom at Eastern Senior High School. Linda and her students were featured on Good Morning America, showcasing the Careers through Culinary Arts Program (CCAP).
L-R Chef Julia Child, Chef Bill Snell of Marriott Corporation, cookbook author and CCAP founder Richard Grausman, Linda.

In February 1996 Linda was selected by the International Program Branch of the Division of Student Services, DC Public Schools to accompany 50 DCPS students on an exchange program to Russia. The trip was enlightening and interesting for all. In exchange, a Russian teacher came to America and stayed with Linda while she visited schools in Washington, DC.

Just prior to the Christmas holidays, Linda has held classes at her home on Nicholson Street, teaching children how to make and decorate gingerbread houses. Parents bring their children from all over—Chevy Chase, MD; Potomac, MD; and DC.

In 1984 Linda published her book, *Secondhand Shopping in Washington, DC and suburban Maryland: A Guide to over 80 Outlets for Previously Owned Clothing and Other Items, with Tips on Buying, Selling, and Donating Goods*, published by Prudent Publishers and is available in three local libraries. The book is listed on the Internet. I have a tape of her shows on television when she discussed her book and also demonstrated some cooking procedures.

In 2001, Linda decided she wanted to leave the classroom and decided to apply and attend library school. She completed her Masters in Library Science at Catholic University in 2004, then took a job as a School Library Media Specialist at Parkland Middle School in Montgomery County where she still enjoys teaching research and library skills. [Retired 2013!]

CHAPTER 13

THE HUSBAND OF
LINDA CRICHLOW WHITE
ERIC HERBERT WHITE

Eric Herbert White was born in Brooklyn, New York, on September 2, 1950. He was the oldest child of Mark and Irene White. Eric attended elementary school on Crown Street in Brooklyn. He graduated from Lefferts Junior High School in 1963. In June 1968 he received his diploma from Erasmus Hall High School in Brooklyn where he had participated in several activities including the Glee Club. Eric was a member of Siloam Presbyterian Church in Brooklyn and sang in the junior choir there.

He began his college education in 1968 at City College of New York where he majored in history and communications. He received his bachelor of science degree from City College in 1973. Eric enrolled at Columbia University in New York City in 1974 to study for a master of science degree. He was not required to write a dissertation but instead worked on a project entitled "Cable TV—How to Use Public Access." He received his master's degree in library science from Columbia University in June 1975.

Eric with parents, Mark and Irene, and sisters Crystal, Loverna, and Debra, ca. 1986.

Eric and his sisters l-r Debra, Loverna, Crystal and mother Irene, Easter 1966

During the summer of 1974, Eric traveled to Guyana, a country on the northern coast of South America, with a group sponsored by the Black History Department of City College, New York. He spent five weeks there working on community projects. In August 1975 he came to Washington, DC. He was living with his cousin, Stanley White (Ayokunle Odeleye) in the 6400 block of 14th Street, NW. When I met him in 1975 "Ayo" was teaching art at Howard University. He was putting on an art show of his work at the time that I met Eric, and Eric invited me to the show. I have a work of Ayo's art hanging on one of the walls in my home. I cannot call them paintings, because he used several styles of art. Linda and Eric have some large pieces of sculpture at their home that were done by Ayo. At the present time, Ayo is professor of art at Kennesaw State University, located about thirty miles northwest of Atlanta, Georgia.

Eric was appointed browsing room supervisor, Founders Library, Howard University, in the fall of 1975. He later worked as a reference librarian and then "opened" the newly created Audio Visual Division in 1981. He worked at Howard until May of 1991 when he accepted a position as chief of the audio-visual division at the Martin Luther King, Jr., Library at 9th and G Streets, NW, Washington, DC. Eric was given a wonderful goodbye celebration by the library staff at Howard before he left to begin his new job.

Eric and Linda lived at 744 Girard Street, NW. In 1980 they moved to 1335 Madison Street, NW, and in 1992 to Nicholson Street, where they presently reside. Eric has been a very nice son-in-law. Martin was fond of him and so am I. Their first child, Kwame Omar White was born on August 14, 1982. Their second child, Khalila Namtasha, was born on March 7, 1984. As I write this, Kwame is nineteen and Khalila is seventeen; two lovely teenagers.

Eric has been very active in various organizations. He served a term as President of the DC Chapter of Tots and Teens of which he, Linda, Kwame, and Khalila are members. By 1975, thirty chapters of Tots and Teens had been organized throughout the United States. It is an excellent group that offers parents and their children opportunities to get together for worthwhile social and educational activities. Mary Jane Tyler, a long-time friend of ours, is a charter member. The Tots and Teens sponsored their 50th reunion at the Kellogg Center, Gallaudet College, on November 18, 2001. Eric worked faithfully with the group to see that it was a gala affair. Khalila and another member, Hanim Samara, presided at the reunion.

Eric is an excellent photographer and has videotaped many events. Eric is a member of Mount Carmel Baptist Church and has served on the audio-visual committee there. One of his duties is working in the audio booth some Sundays, taping the sermons and messages of the speakers at the church services.

Eric is part of a large family, with lots of cousins, especially on his father's side. He has three sisters, Crystal, Debra, and Loverna. At the present time his parents, Mark and Irene, live in a lovely home in Annapolis, St. Claire, Maryland. Deborah lives in Detroit. (Mark White had 18 sisters and brothers. See the *The Whitehead Family Book* listed in For Further Reading)

Eric, Linda, Kwame, and Khalila at the White Family
Reunion in Los Angeles, California 2007.

Eric & Linda 2004

CHAPTER 14

CHILDREN OF LINDA AND ERIC WHITE

KWAME OMAR ASOMANI WHITE

Kwame, the son of Eric and Linda White, was born on Saturday, August 14, 1982. He was born at Howard University Hospital and weighed 6 pounds, 5 ounces. He was a beautiful baby. I remember when Martha (my sister-in-law) and I went to the hospital to see the new baby she said, "Marietta, he is precious." We all thought the same thing then and we all think the same thing now.

I would baby sit with him from time to time. I remember strolling with him inside the Safeway store one day and a customer at the store asked me if I would stay in the aisle until she locate her friend who was also in the store. When they both came back, she asked her friend, "Have you ever seen such a pretty baby in all of your life?" Truly, Kwame was a "pretty" baby. We enjoyed having him when Linda and Eric would bring him to our house. He was a pleasant, cheerful child.

Kwame attended Howard pre-School sponsored by a church located at Piney Branch Road near Georgia Avenue, NW. He started kindergarten at Shepherd Elementary School located at 7800 14th Street, NW. His teacher was Miss Wendy Bridges. She was a very concerned young lady.

Miss Bridges later joined Mount Carmel Church where I am a member and I found out that she is the granddaughter of one of the oldest and most admired members of the church, Mrs. Minnette Taliaferro. Miss Bridges took her class to Eastern High School one day after Linda had invited them for a cookie-making lesson in her classroom.

Linda and Eric transferred Kwame and Khalila to St. Michael's Catholic School, 824 Wayne Avenue, Silver Spring, Maryland, where he started the third grade. When Kwame was ready to go to the sixth grade, he entered the middle school at St. John's College High School at 27th and Military Road, NW.

While he was on the elementary level, Kwame participated in lots of activities. He took piano lessons from Dr. Vivian McBrier, who had been a professor at the University of the District of Columbia as well as at other schools. She lived at 1735 Shepherd Street, NW, and held piano recitals at her home every year. Dr. McBrier was originally from Lynchburg, Virginia, and had taught music at the school where my cousins Edwina, Carolyn, and Edward (Sonny) attended.

Dr. McBrier showed me a picture of her with the class that Edwina was in as a student. She said she had always admired my mother's sister, Mildred. They had attended the same church in Lynchburg.

Kwame and Khalila at one of Dr. Vivian McBrier's Christmas piano recitals

Kwame played soccer and seemed to like it a lot. Eric's parents and I attended one of his games. Kwame also liked to perform magic tricks; he was really good at it.

He put on a magic show at the Martin Luther King, Jr., Library for a group of children. He and Khalila, his "assistant", also put on a magic show at the Stoddard Baptist Nursing Home for some of the elderly people there.

Kwame graduated from St. John's High School in 2000 (A millennial!) and attended Kent State University majoring in aviation flight. He later transferred to N.C.A&T where Khalila was where he majored in transportation logistics, made the honor roll, and earned a scholarship! Kwame graduated from A&T in 2006.

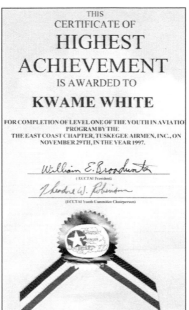

Kwame also participated in the Youth in Aviation program sponsored by the East Coast Chapter of the Tuskegee Airmen and learned to fly an airplane.

KHALILA NAMTASHA WHITE

A few lines about my granddaughter, Khalila Namtasha White, daughter of Eric and Linda White.

It is a real pleasure for me to look back over the years and think about some of the very nice things that Khalila has done. She was born at Howard University Hospital on March 7, 1984. On June 18, 1984, Khalila was christened at Shiloh Baptist Church in Alexandria, Virginia, by the Rev. Moses W. Beasley, pastor, our long-time family friend.

Khalila attended Shepherd Elementary School on 14th St., NW, transferred to St. Michael's School on Wayne Avenue in Silver Spring; attended Jefferson Junior High School and graduated from Wilson High School in June 2002. From Wilson she attended Bennett College in Greensboro, NC, then later transferred to North Carolina A&T State University (the same school Jesse Jackson had attended) in Greensboro, North Carolina. She graduated in June 2006 with a bachelor of science degree in business merchandising. She has taken courses at Trinity College.

During her early years, Khalila took piano lessons from Dr. Vivian McBrier who lived at 1735 Shepherd Street, NW, and played on various programs sponsored by Dr. McBrier and also at Mt. Carmel Baptist Church. Khalila had taken part in the nursery school and primary program at Mt. Carmel and other activities. She joined as a member of Mt. Carmel when she was about eight years old.

About 1990, I had attended a picnic at the home of Elsie Breeding Ford (Granville's first wife) (with Linda, Eric Kwame, and Khalila.) There was a large swimming pool in their back area. As I looked around, I was surprised to see Khalila (about 6 years old) swim the length of the pool and back without hesitation. She

Linda: We sent Kwame and Khalila to Beauvoir School summer camp where they had a great swimming program as part of the summer lessons. Both Kwame and Khalila learned to swim at Beauvoir but Khalila really took to the water like a fish...maybe because she's a Pisces!

Eric, Khalila, and Kwame in the pool at the Silver Spring YMCA ca. 1990. This photo was used in one of the "Y" publications.

is an expert swimmer. I knew she had attended summer camp (Camp Atwater, in Massachusetts), but I did not know that she had learned to swim so well. As the years passed, she worked as a lifeguard during the summer at Rollingcrest Pool in Hyattsville, Maryland, at some of the D.C. public pools and at Tenley Sport and Health Club.

During the summer of 2005 Khalila went with Crossroads Africa to Ghana, West Africa, where she did volunteer work for six weeks, training and teaching the children there. She has also been to Niger, Africa, where she and Linda visited Khalila's godfather, Dr. Reggie Simmons, who was working in Niger for Africare.

Khalila graduated from A&T in 2006 and took a job in D.C. at Nordstrom company. Over the years, Khalila has become an expert at sewing and art work. She has made many lovely handbags and paintings. Some of her paintings are hanging on the walls at my house.

Linda ca. 1953 wearing a jumper that Aunt Beth (Elizabeth Lee) had made for her with hand embroidery on the straps. In 1987, Khalila is wearing the same jumper; Marietta had saved it!
A jumper was a skirt with straps and was fashionable for ladies in the 1950s and 60s. Marietta used to lament the fact that she had a hard time finding "Colored" dolls for Linda back when she was growing up. Times changed and Khalila had lots!

Khalila in Lake Arrowhead, in Luray, VA, where Aunt Beth and Uncle Clyde lived, ca. 1993

Linda, Marietta, and Khalila in about 2005.

EPILOGUE

Stevens, Garland, and Glover descendants have strong roots in the Lynchburg, Virginia, area but now live all over the world. Some locales with the highest numbers are the Washington, DC; Pittsburgh, Pennsylvania; and Boston, Massachusetts, areas. They became buyers for department stores, beauticians, ministers, teachers, government and public officials, and military officers. One of James and Lucy Glover's great-great-great-grandchildren, Jay Wynne, lives in London where he is a BBC weather forecaster.

Jerusalem Baptist Church is still in existence as is Mt. Carmel Baptist in Washington although neither has a congregation as large as those in the 1940s and 1950s. Howard University and Hampton are still operating. Hampton changed from Institute to a University in 1984 but is still the "home by the sea" to thousands of alumni and is one of the few historically Black colleges and universities operating in the "Black."

The story herein is not just of Marietta's family but of all African American families. As Henry Louis Gates states, we have achieved despite the odds. Over the years, the extended family that began with the Glovers, Garlands, and Stevenses in central Virginia has not been an especially closely knit one but there are many ties that bind us. To borrow from John Baker, Jr., author of *The Washingtons of Wessyngton Plantation*, this story, like his, is a tribute to those who came before and, a beacon of hope to those who follow. To be continued…

APPENDIX

To illustrate how genealogy research is often done, we are including some family documents and some documents from Ancestry.com that helped to pull the pieces together. These documents include census pages, wills, death notices, and magazine and newspaper articles. Even though some documents were included within the initial narrative, some additional material appears here in the Appendix. We hope other family members will use these and similar documents for further research.

Appendix A

Some documents related to Marietta Stevens Crichlow ancestry.

Marietta Crichlow Family Documents

MARIETTA STEVENS CRICHLOW
PATERNAL LINEAGE

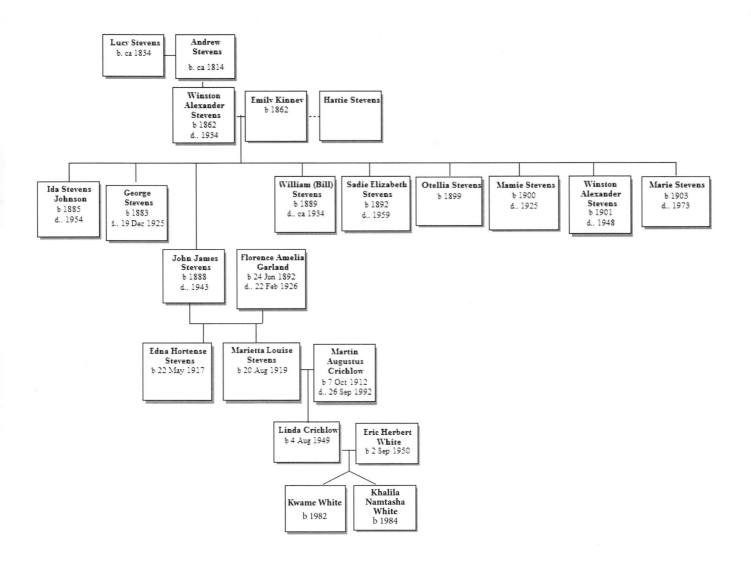

MARIETTA STEVENS CRICHLOW
MATERNAL LINEAGE

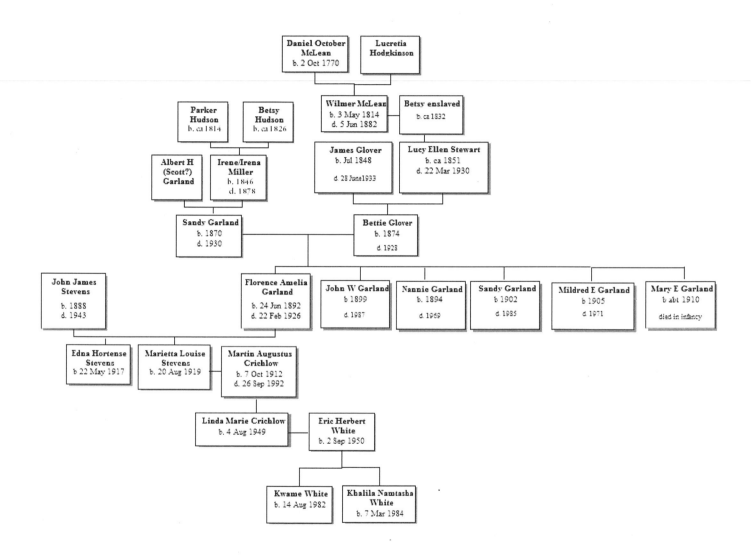

DEATH NOTICE FOR
MARY ETTA KINNEY, THE RELATIVE FOR
WHOM MARIETTA WAS NAMED
TUESDAY, JANUARY 4, 1927

KINNEY. Departed this life January 1, 1927, at 11:55 p.m., at her residence, 624 24th st. n.w., MARY ETTA KINNEY. She is survived by two brothers, relatives and friends. Funeral from Nineteenth Street Baptist Church Wednesday, 2 p.m. Remains resting at Moon & Allen's funeral parlors, 11 Florida ave. n.w. 4*

KINNEY. The Golden Leaf Whispering Hope Society announces the death of Mrs. MARY KINNEY. Funeral Wednesday, January 5, 2 p.m., from Nineteenth Street Baptist Church, 10th and Eye sts. n.w.
MRS. PAULINE MARSHALL, Pres.
MARIE L. JOHNSON, Rec. Sec. •

KINNEY. The Ladies' Reliable Immediate Relief Society are requested to meet at the Nineteenth Street Baptist Church Wednesday, 1 o'clock p.m., to attend the funeral of MARY E. KINNEY.
REBECCA BRENT, President.
A. C. GREEN, Recording Sec.

KINNEY. The Ladies' Cliff Rock Society announces the death of Mrs. MARY KINNEY. Funeral Wednesday, January 5, 1927, from Nineteenth Street Baptist Church at 2 p.m.
PAULINE MARSHALL, President.
JENNIE E. BARNES, Financial Secretary.

KINNEY. The Col. Charles Young Women's Relief Association, announces the death of Mrs. MARY KINNEY. Funeral Wednesday, January 5, 1927, from Nineteenth Street Baptist Church at 2 p.m.
PAULINE MARSHALL, Pres.
MARY E. BOWMAN, Rec. Sec.,

KINNEY. The members of the Ladies' Banneker Aid Association are requested to attend the funeral of Miss MARY E. KINNEY, Wednesday, January 5, 1927, at 2 p.m., from Nineteenth Street Baptist Church.
MAMIE A. TAPSCOTT, Pres.
LANDONIA FULSOME, Rec. Secy.

To illustrate how genealogy research is often done, we are including the will and newspaper death notices of Mary Etta Kinney, the person after whom Marietta was named. Apparently Aunt Mary was a very active, dedicated church and community worker. She also had been organized enough to plan her estate and write a will, something that probably not many Colored women did at that time. Her will, on page 129, lists some of her relatives. Her death notices, which were published in the Washington Evening Star indicate some of the organizations she belonged to.

WILL OF MARY ETTA KINNEY

Last Will and Testament

OF

══════════════ MARY E. KINNEY ══════════════

In the Name of God, Amen.

I, MARY E. KINNEY of Washington, D. C.

──────being of sound and disposing mind, memory and understanding, considering the certainty of death and the uncertainty of the time thereof, and being desirous to settle my worldly affairs, and thereby be the better prepared to leave this world when it shall please the Almighty to call me hence, do therefore make and publish this my last Will and Testament, hereby revoking and annulling all wills by me heretofore made, in manner and form following, that is to say:

First, and principally, I commit my soul into the hands of Almighty God, and my body to the earth, to be decently buried at the discretion of my executor........ hereinafter named; and my will is, that all my just debts and funeral expenses shall be paid by my executor........ hereinafter named as soon after my decease as shall be convenient;

Second, I give, devise and bequeath to Elizabeth Proctor, who has been more than a sister to me, all my bedroom furniture not otherwise disposed of, all bedding of whatever kind, such table silver as I may have, all my pictures and portraits, my two trunks, all my linen of whatever kind, and all my clothing not otherwise disposed of.────────

THIRD, I give, devise and bequeath to my friend, Purcell Worrell, of 922 Twenty-fourth Street, N. W., this city, my Hudson seal coat, my wardrobe which sets in my bedroom, and all clothing contained in it at the time of my death.────────

FOURTH, I give, devise and bequeath to my niece, Alma Kinney Clarkson of Arrington, Nelson County, Virginia, Four Hundred Dollars ($400) in cash.────────

FIFTH, I give, devise and bequeath to my niece, Josephine Kinney, daughter of James Chapman Kinney, Four Hundred Dollars ($400) in cash.──

SIXTH, I give, devise and bequeath to my half-brother, James Chapman Kinney, of Arrington, Nelson County, Virginia, One Hundred Dollars ($100) in cash.────────

SEVENTH, I give, devise and bequeath to my half-brother, John J. Kinney of Mt. Carmel, West Virginia, One Hundred Dollars ($100) in cash.──

EIGHTH, I give, devise and bequeath to my two grand-nieces, Marietta Stevens and Edna Hortense Stevens, minor children of John Stevens of 2024 Fourth Street, N. W. this city, each the following; to Marietta one (1) diamond-chip breast pin and Fifty Dollars ($50) in cash, to Edna Hortense one (1) diamond-chip breast pin and Fifty Dollars ($50) in cash.────────

NINTH, I give, devise and bequeath to my grand-nieces, Odell Clarkson and Zoa Clarkson, minor children of Alma Kinney Clarkson above referred to, each the follwoing: to Odell one (1) Fifty Dollar U. S. Liberty Bond, to Zoa one (1) Fifty Dollar U. S. Liberty Bond.────────

OVER

Linda: I don't know any Kinney or Clarkson cousins but some of them are likely still in Nelson County. We've got to search for them. Remember from Chapter 2, Emily Kinney Stevens was Marietta's paternal grandmother.

Sheet #2.

TENTH,

I give, devise and bequeath to the 19th Street Baptist Church of this city One Hundred Dollars ($100) in cash. _____

ELEVENTH, I give, devise and bequeath to the Ladies' Christian Mite Society of the 19th Street Baptist Church above mentioned Fifty Dollars ($50) in cash. _____

TWELFTH, I direct that all monies due me from the following benevolent and fraternal organizations:

Colonel Charles Young Women's Relief Association,
Ladies' Cliff Rock Society,
Ladies' Golden Leaf Whispering Hope Society,
Ladies' Reliable Relief Association,
Ladies' Banneker Relief Association,
Shamrock House Hold of Ruth, G. U. O. of O. F.,
Women's Frederick Douglass Benefit Association,
Young Ladies' Immediate Relief Association,

be paid to my executor hereinafter named to be applied by him as follows; first to the payment of my funeral expenses and the remainder to be distributed to legatees according to the terms of my will.

Thirteenth, I am the owner of twenty (20) shares of stock of the National Benefit Life Insurance Company of Washington, D.C. and I give and bequeath ten (10) of those shares to Odell and Zoa Blackson, share and share alike and I give and bequeath to Marietta and Edna Hortens Stevens ten (10) of those shares, share and share alike. _____

136

All the rest and residue of my estate, both real, personal and mixed, I give, devise, and bequeath to my...niece, Alma Kinney Clarkson...
TO HER, her heirs and assigns for ever...

....and...

to them and their heirs and assigns forever, share and share alike, as tenants in common.

And Lastly, I do hereby nominate, constitute and appoint my...friend Archibald S. Pinkett..execut.or...of this, my last Will and Testament, and I desire that my execut.or...........hereinbefore named shall not be required to give bond for the faithful performance of the duties of that office.

In Testimony Whereof, I have set my hand and seal to this, my last Will and Testament, at.........Washington, D. C..........................this........twenty-eighth..........day of............December...........in the year of our Lord one thousand nine hundred and...twenty-six...

Mary E. Kinney [SEAL]

Signed, Sealed, Published, and Declared, by...Mary E. Kinney.........................
...........................the above-named testa.rix., as and for h..er last Will and Testament, in our presence, and at h.er. request, and in h.er. presence, and in the presence of each other, we have hereunto subscribed our names as attesting witnesses.

Edmond W. Scott

Residence *1447 S St. nw.*

Mary Edith Harley

Residence *924 - 24 St n.W.*
(Write very plainly)

137

NATIONAL BENEFIT LIFE INSURANCE

Among Marietta's memorabilia was a certificate for 10 shares of the capital stock of the National Benefit Life Insurance Company that had been issued to Mary Etta Kinney in 1924 and transferred to John Stevens for Marietta and Edna following Kinney's death in 1927. Unfortunately, the certificate has no value today because the company did not survive the Depression. Following is a story about insurance companies that shows how hard Black folks, despite tenuous resources, tried to help our communities.

The following, extracted from an article about African American Insurance Companies mentions S. W. Rutherford whose signature is on the certificate. See images next page.

Insurance Companies, African American–Owned

The development of African American insurance companies in the late nineteenth and twentieth centuries is attributable to the need to provide stable financial assistance to African American families in times of need. Prior to the appearance of insurance companies, fraternal orders and mutual aid societies provided a primary means of charitable relief to widows, orphans, and those with health problems. Over time these charitable societies failed because they neglected to incorporate benefit structures that accounted for the risks associated with insuring policyholders. Conversely, with surplus capital from improved business management and instilled with a sense of dedication to racial progress, African American insurance companies became centers for institutional development and expanded the range of social services offered within African American communities.

African American insurance companies perceived honesty and integrity with respect to the payment of beneficiary policies as the most imperative business ethic during the initial years of their development. This profound desire to prove that African Americans were capable in business led several of these African American insurance companies to provide support in the form of loans and counsel to each other during times of trouble. In the final analysis, however, these businesses rose and fell like all other American businesses: on the uncertain winds of market conditions.

In 1898, S. W. Rutherford of Washington, D.C., embarked on a personal mission to create a mutual aid society that would provide benefits to African American families in times of sickness and death; his association became known as the National Benefit Life Insurance Company. With a small staff and minimal amount of office space, the company managed to remain afloat during its formative years. By 1919 this business had become a self-sustaining and profitable enterprise. Rutherford sold $100,000 of capital stock in the company that year alone, and National Benefit organized its benefits structure on a legal reserve basis. Looking to take full advantage of this success, in 1923 its board of directors sought to expand the company's operations in nine new states. The directors increased the company's capital stock to $250,000 to finance this decision. Unfortunately, there were not enough investors to purchase the sale of its stock, and several of the leading officials within the company had to take out personal loans to keep the business afloat.

Crawford, Malachi D. *Insurance Companies, African American–Owned* Encyclopedia of African American History, 1896 to the Present: From the Age of Segregation to the Twenty-first Century, edited by Ed. Paul Finkelman. Oxford African American Studies Center, http://www.oxfordaasc.com (accessed 8 April 2014).

This stock certificate was purchased by Aunt Mary Etta Kinney in 1924 and signed over to Marietta and Edna but lost its value during the Great Depression when the company went out of business.

WHO WAS WILMER MCLEAN?

Linda wants to document that Wilmer McLean was the father of her great-great-grandmother Lucy Glover. That would make Wilmer McLean Linda's great-great-great-grandfather.

Note the resemblance between Lucy and Wilmer. Through family oral history and documents we can place Lucy at both Manassas and Appomattox at the time that Wilmer lived in both places. We still have more research to do to prove the connection.

Wilmer McLean

From: http://en.wikipedia.org/
wiki/Wilmer_McLean

Lucy Glover with her daughter
Bettie Glover Garland (left), granddaughter Florence Garland Stevens
and baby Edna Stevens ca. 1917.

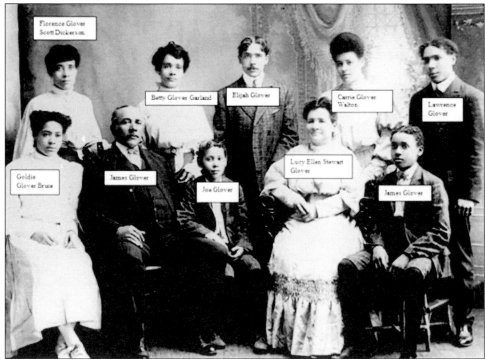

James and Lucy Glover family ca. 1900

Wilmer McLean—First Battle of Bull Run

Early in the Civil War, on July 21, 1861, what would become the First Battle of Bull Run took place on the farm of Wilmer McLean in Manassas, Prince William County, Virginia. Union Army artillery fired at McLean's house, which was being used as a headquarters for Confederate Brigadier General P. G. T. Beauregard, and a cannonball dropped through the kitchen fireplace.

McLean was a retired major in the Virginia militia, but at 47, he was too old to return to active duty at the outbreak of the Civil War. He made his living during the war as a sugar broker supplying the Confederate States Army. He decided to move because his commercial activities were centered mostly in southern Virginia and the Union army presence in his area of northern Virginia made his work difficult. He undoubtedly was also motivated by a desire to protect his family from a repetition of their combat experience. In the spring of 1863, he and his family moved about 120 miles south to Appomattox County, Virginia, to the community called Appomattox Court House.

Appomattox Court House

On April 9, 1865, the war revisited Wilmer McLean. Confederate General Robert E. Lee was about to surrender to Lieutenant General Ulysses S. Grant. He sent a messenger to Appomattox Court House to find a place to meet. On April 8, 1865, the messenger knocked on McLean's door and requested the use of his home, to which McLean reluctantly agreed. Lee surrendered to Grant in the parlor of McLean's house, effectively ending the Civil War. Later, McLean is supposed to have said "The war began in my front yard and ended in my front parlor."

from Wikipedia

Stories passed down through the Glover family tell that our ancestors (Lucy and her mother Betsy, and others) were there in Manassas in 1861 and also at Appomattox Court House in 1865 when Lee surrendered to Grant.

Wilmer McLean's home in Appomattox 1865, soon after Lee's surrender to Grant

Carolyn Brown and Linda in front of the house in April 2013.

As indicated on page 16, Glover-Garland family stories report that Lucy Glover was the daughter of Wilmer McLean and an enslaved woman, Betsy Love. Indeed, photos of Wilmer McLean and Grandma Lucy indicate a very close resemblance. Although her death certificate lists a Henry Stewart as her father, family members and historians today say that "they just wouldn't" have listed McLean as her father back there then. Importantly, we can "place" her in Manassas and Appomattox. Both Aunt Goldie and Connie, as well as others wrote about their mother having been born in Manassas. Grandpa Glover's death certificate does confirm that he was born in Appomattox. Lucy and James must have married about 1870 and moved to Lynchburg where their children were born and raised until the family moved to Boston in 1900.

A 2013 exhibit at the Lynchburg Legacy Museum included several items that our cousin Carolyn Brown provided. Part of the exhibit included this tag:

> ## "We were at Manassas and Appomattox"
> Many African American families trace their ancestors' presence back to and before the Civil War. Sisters Carolyn Brown and Edwina Brown Beverley, for example, are descended from the enslaved Stewart family, held in bondage by Wilmer McLean, who had moved southwest from Manassas to get out of the way of the war. A family story recorded what happened the day cannonballs was fired at the McLean house and came down the chimney but did not explode. Had it exploded, everyone in the house would have been killed on the spot, but everyone lived, going on to make their lives in the New South. The Browns' ancestors' names appear in Lynchburg's city directories from the 1870s onward. Family members owned businesses, raised children, garnered education, served churches, and taught others, even until today.

Family members are hoping that one day there will be a similar display tag at Appomattox.

One might ask why we want to document this relationship. An article about an African American Woman who became a member of the D.A.R. (Daughters of the American Revolution) stated that "black family history such as Raney's is unearthed, traced and documented, historians said. It's rarer still when it's linked to a storied family with power, privilege and a celebrated legacy." McLean didn't necessarily have power but he is associated with the event that helped free the slaves—Lee's surrender to Grant at Appomattox.

Most genealogists and historians rejoice when they are able to pinpoint the plantation where their family once lived. Despite the enslaved history, it is still our history and needs to be documented.

Linda, husband Eric, and cousin Carolyn Brown of Lynchburg visited Appomattox in March of 2013. When they were there, after the park historian Patrick Schroeder reminded us of McLean's Scotch-Irish heritage, Cousin Carolyn told how her niece (our cousin) Marla had visited the doctor recently and was told that the condition she had was normally seen in people of Scottish descent! So, family genealogy is useful not just for the family history but also for health reasons. One of the most important uses of history is to help predict the future and avoid the mistakes of the past. Therefore if we know our health history, we can avoid some otherwise inherited diseases.

In addition, when people are looking for their roots, it often takes us to the farm or plantation of our (white) ancestors. We are still researching our roots and hope that other family members will join in and continue the quest. It must be noted, too, that even though we are referring in this book to some previously "enslaved" ancestors, we still have not located documents that confirm that our ancestors before Emancipation were all enslaved.

Glover family photo on display at Lynchburg Legacy Museum April 2013

More research remains to be done!
Pictured: Linda and cousin Carolyn Brown with Patrick Schroeder, Historian, Appomattox Court House National Historical Park

·

Contact information as of March 2014:
Patrick A. Schroeder, Historian
Appomattox Court House National Historical Park
P. O. Box 218
Appomattox, VA, 24522
434-352-8987 Ext. 232
434-352-8330 Fax
patrick_schroeder@nps.gov
http://www.nps.gov/apco/index.htm

Informant's Surname, Informant's First Name; Slave's Name;
Mother's Name; Date of Birth; Place of Birth

MCLEAN, SEE: MCCLAIN, MCLAIN
McLean, Virginia B; Henry; Betsy; 1858; Prince William
McLean, Virginia B; John Alexander; Betsey; Jul 15, 1856; Prince William
McLean, Virginia B; Maria; Mary Ann; Oct 30, 1856; Prince William
McLean, Virginia B; Rachael; Mary Ann; 1858; Prince William
McLean, Wilmer; (fem); Mary Ann; Oct 5, 1853; Prince William
McLean, Wilmer; (male); Betsey; Dec 1855; Prince William
McLearen, James; James Rosser; Sarah; Oct 1854; Fauquier

p. 108

To the right is a listing of children born to slaves of Wilmer and/or wife, Virginia McLean between 1853 and 1865.

Below is the 1860 Census Slave Schedule where we have "matched" names to personal descriptions. Allowing for some discrepancy in census recording, the names and birthdates match the people who are listed in the 1860 and 1870 Lynchburgh census.

This data is from when Wilmer was still living in Prince William County. We are still researching the proof of Betsy, Henry and Lucy at Appomattox. Family accounts report that Betsy was a cook in the Mclean house and that Lucy was just old enough to help out. In addition, it is said that Lucy was treated like a member of the (Mc-Lean) family and often played with the McLean children.

The story of Wilmer's move from Manassas to Appomattox is well known. We are surmising that Lucy and Betsy moved with the McLeans to Manassas in 1863. Because Betsy's husband is noted as Henry in several documents and because a child of Betsy was named Henry in 1858, it is believed that Betsy and Henry were "a couple" legal or otherwise, before 1858. We are still looking for that proof.

ancestry.com | 1860 U.S. Federal Census - Slave Schedules

◄ | Virginia ＞ Prince William ＞ Not Stated 　Related Content

1870 Census showing Henry and Betsey Stewart living in Lynchburg

Page No. 47

SCHEDULE 1.—Inhabitants in _Eastern Division_, in the County of _Campbell_, State of _Virginia_, enumerated by me on the _22d_ day of _June_, 1870;

Post Office _Lynchburg_

16	366	391	Stewart Henry	35	m	B	Brakeman
17			— Betsey	30	f	m	Washer & Ironer
18			— Lucie	21	f	m	"
19			— Isaac	23	m	m	Works on Rail Road
20			— Henry	12	m	B	attending School
21			— John	6	m	B	"
22			— William	4	m	B	at Home
23			— Hannah	1	f	B	"

Below: 1880 Census showing Bessie Stewart living with her children James and Lucy are living next door with their three oldest children.

Note A.—The Census Year begins June 1, 1879, and ends May 31, 1880.

Note B.—All persons will be included in the Enumeration who were living on the 1st day of June, 1880. No others will. Children BORN SINCE June 1, 1880, will be OMITTED. Members of Families who have DIED SINCE June 1, 1880, will be INCLUDED.

Note C.—Questions Nos. 13, 14, 22 and 23 are not to be asked in respect to persons under 10 years of age.

Inhabitants in _Lynchburg_, in the County of _Campbell_, State of _Virginia_ enumerated by me on the _____ day of June, 1880.

Stewart Bessie	mu f 45		1		Servant
— Horace	B m 21	Son	1		Laborer
— John	B m 20	Son	1		Laborer
— William	B m 18	Son	1		Laborer
— James	B m 9	Son	1		at School
— Bessie	B f 11	Daught.	1		at School
Glover James	B m 34		1		Huckster
— Lucy	mu f 28	wife	1		Keeps House
— Ouie	mu f 8	Daught.	1		at School
— Florence	mu f 6	Daughter	1		
— Elijah	mu m 2	Son	1		

A newspaper article from the Lynchburg Daily News Jan 21, 1874 reported that Henry Stewart died in a railroad accident.

By 1881, Betsy is listed in the Lynchburg City Directory as living on Lynch between 19th and 20th, the same address given for her son-in-law James Glover so presumably she had gone to live with her daughter and son-in-law.

Bessie/Betsy Stewart in 1880 Census . In various documents the name is spelled Betsy, Betsey or Bessie. The last name is sometimes spelled Steward.

DEATH CERTIFICATES FOR JAMES AND LUCY GLOVER

Marietta's maternal great-grandparents

The death certificate lists Henry Stewart, Betsy's husband, as Lucy's father. Family members believe that was the "polite" recording and that Wilmer McLean was Lucy's birth father.

JAMES GLOVER'S
FREEDMAN'S BANK SIGNATURE REGISTER

The Freedman's Savings and Trust Company (often called the Freedman's Bank) was created by Congress in 1865 to assist newly freed slaves and African American soldiers at the end of the Civil War. There were 37 offices in 17 states and the District of Columbia. The bank failed in 1874 and many depositors lost their savings, but the records of the bank remain. Among the records are the registers of signatures of depositors. The registers show the names, residence, and description of each depositor. They may also include the genealogy and relatives of the depositor. Most depositors were African Americans. A few were European immigrants mostly in New York City. James Glover's register, from August 1871 shows his wife, Lucy and brothers, Linus, Edmund and Harvey. (To date, this is the only evidence we have of any siblings of James Glover.) The original records of the Freedman's Bank are housed at the National Archive facility in College Park, MD but have been digitized and are available in several on-line resources.

SOURCE: Ancestry.com. Freedman's Bank Records, 1865-1871 [database on-line]. Provo, UT, USA: Ancestry.com Operations Inc, 2005.

DEATH CERTIFICATES FOR SANDY GARLAND AND BETTY GLOVER GARLAND

Marietta's maternal grandparents

First certificate (No. 25313):

CERTIFICATE OF DEATH
COMMONWEALTH OF VIRGINIA
DEPARTMENT OF HEALTH
BUREAU OF VITAL STATISTICS

1 PLACE OF DEATH — COUNTY OF Campbell — CITY OF Lynchburg — (No. 1804 Main Street, St. Third Ward)

2 FULL NAME Sandy Asbury Garland
(A) RESIDENCE No. 1804 Main Street, St. Third Ward

3 SEX Male — 4 COLOR OR RACE Colored — 5 Widowed
5A WIFE OF Bettie G. Garland
6 DATE OF BIRTH 1870
7 AGE 60 Years
8 TRADE Minister
9 INDUSTRY Baptist Church
10 DATE LAST WORKED Aug. 1930
12 BIRTHPLACE Amherst County, Virginia
13 NAME Albert H. Garland
14 BIRTHPLACE Virginia
15 MAIDEN NAME Irene Garland
16 BIRTHPLACE Virginia
17 INFORMANT Mrs. Mildred Brown, 1715 Bedford Ave.
18 BURIAL Cemetery Date 11/11/30
19 UNDERTAKER J. H. Wilson Co. Inc., 505 Fifth Street
20 FILED Nov. 11, 1930 Grace Davidson, Registrar

21 DATE OF DEATH Nov. 7th, 1930

This is to certify that this is a true and correct reproduction of the original record filed with the Bureau of Vital Statistics, Virginia Department of Health, Richmond, Virginia.

APR 3 1979
Date Issued

DEANE HUXTABLE, State Registrar

ANY REPRODUCTION OF THIS DOCUMENT IS PROHIBITED BY STATUTE.
DO NOT ACCEPT UNLESS ON SAFETY PAPER WITH IMPRESSED SEAL OF THE BUREAU OF VITAL STATISTICS CLEARLY AFFIXED.

Section 32-353.27, Code of Virginia, as Amended.

Second certificate (No. 8008):

CERTIFICATE OF DEATH
COMMONWEALTH OF VIRGINIA
BUREAU OF VITAL STATISTICS
STATE BOARD OF HEALTH

1 PLACE OF DEATH — COUNTY OF Campbell — CITY OF Lynchburg — (No. 1804 Main St., St. 3d Ward)

2 FULL NAME Bettie G Garland
(A) RESIDENCE No. 1804 Main St., St. 3d Ward

3 SEX female — 4 COLOR OR RACE col — 5 Married
5A HUSBAND OF Rev. S. A. Garland
6 DATE OF BIRTH
7 AGE about 55
8 OCCUPATION Domestic
9 BIRTHPLACE Lynchburg, Va.
10 NAME OF FATHER James Glover
11 BIRTHPLACE Appomatox, Co. Va.
12 MAIDEN NAME OF MOTHER Lucy Steward
13 BIRTHPLACE OF MOTHER Appomatox, Co. Va.
14 INFORMANT Rev. S. A. Garland, 1804 Main St.
15 FILED April 17, 1928 Elizabeth Sydnor, Registrar

16 DATE OF DEATH April 14th, 1928
17 I HEREBY CERTIFY THAT I ATTENDED DECEASED FROM June 1, 1926 to April 14, 1928
THAT I LAST SAW HER ALIVE ON Apr. 14, 1928
AND THAT DEATH OCCURED ON DATE STATED ABOVE A 5/40 PM
CAUSE OF DEATH Pulmonary Tuberculosis (31) DURATION 31 mos.
(SIGNED) J. H. Brown, M.D. 714 — 5 St.
19 PLACE OF BURIAL Baptist Cemetery — April 17th-28
20 UNDERTAKER Strange & Higginbotham, 909-5th Ave.

This is to certify that this is a true and correct reproduction of the original record filed with the Bureau of Vital Statistics, Virginia Department of Health, Richmond, Virginia.

APR 3 1979
Date Issued

DEANE HUXTABLE, State Registrar

ANY REPRODUCTION OF THIS DOCUMENT IS PROHIBITED BY STATUTE.
DO NOT ACCEPT UNLESS ON SAFETY PAPER WITH IMPRESSED SEAL OF THE BUREAU OF VITAL STATISTICS CLEARLY AFFIXED.

Section 32-353.27, Code of Virginia, as Amended.

APPENDIX B

Some documents related Martin Augustus Crichlow's ancestry.

MARTIN CRICHLOW FAMILY DOCUMENTS

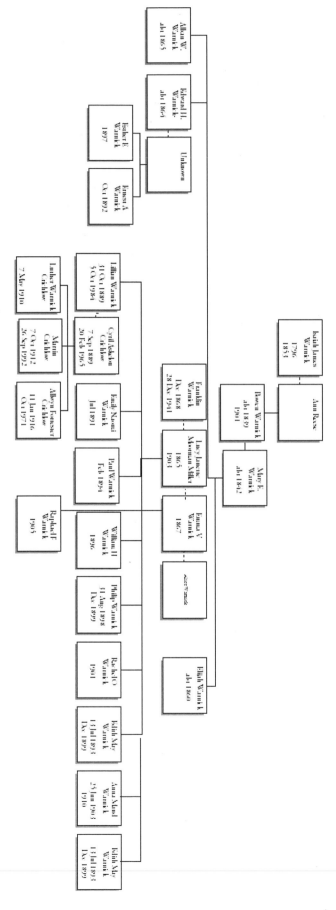

MARTIN AUGUSTUS CRICHLOW LINEAGE

"FOR WORK AMONG COLORED PEOPLE"

Cyril returned to the United States from Liberia in 1921. According to this article, it wasn't long before he became active with the Seventh Day Baptist Church in Detroit, Michigan. The following article provides some of the context around which he came to work in Detroit.

FOR WORK AMONG COLORED PEOPLE

For some time different Seventh Day Baptists have been in communication with individuals and groups of colored people about the beliefs and polity of the Seventh Day Baptist denomination. The interest was so great at the Eastern Association that a Provisional Committee for work among the Colored People was appointed, consisting of Willard D. Burdick, chairman, James L. Skaggs, Ahva J. C. Bond and William L. Burdick.

The plan for securing funds to start the work until one of our denominational societies shall be able to take it over, is for persons to give one dollar a week for a year,—this giving not to interfere with their giving for the New Forward Movement work. The response has been gratifying.

The committee chose James L. Skaggs to serve as secretary-treasurer.

In the interests of this new work the committee arranged with Cyril A. Crichlow to serve as evangelist and field secretary for one year. About enough has been subscribed to provide for the salary.

Mr Crichlow is a native of the island of Trinidad, and has always been a Sabbath-keeper. Mrs. Crichlow was born at Salem,

CYRIL A. CRICHLOW, Field Secretary
209 Prospect Ave., Asbury Park, N. J.

N. J., and from early life has been a Sabbath-keeper. They have three sons: Luther, Martin and Forrester. Both Mr. and Mrs. Crichlow have engaged in mission work, and are experienced teachers. They are non-resident members of the Detroit Seventh Day Baptist Church and are licensed by the church as evangelists.

Mrs. Crichlow is helping to meet the expenses of their rented house by letting out furnished rooms to summer visitors in the city.

It is the purpose of the committee to keep thoroughly acquainted with the progress of the work through correspondence with Mr. Crichlow and others, and, so far as possible, to have monthly meetings with him in the interests of the work. Following out this plan Elders Skaggs and Bond, and Mrs. Burdick and I visited the Crichlows in their home September 26, spending an enjoyable and profitable day with them. We also called Elder Williams from his carpenter work for a few minutes to talk with us, as we passed the building where he was working. Those present at the Eastern Association will recall his making a short talk. He is a loyal and enthusiastic supporter of the work at Asbury Park.

When Mr. and Mrs. Crichlow went to Asbury Park they started a Sabbath school, holding it in their home. Both of them are doing personal work in the city, and are corresponding with a good many people. They have sent out literature to several hundred persons. Some time ago Mr. Crichlow asked me not to have any of the old SABBATH RECORDERS at the Publishing House destroyed, for he wished to use them among his people. We carried about 500 copies to him last Wednesday.

But it is quite impossible for Mr. Crichlow to hold evangelistic and Sabbath meetings in his home with the expectation that people will respond in any considerable numbers. He must have a place for meetings where the people will not excuse themselves from attending because the services are held in a private house.

There are probably 2,000 or 3,000 colored people in Asbury Park. There is a hall nicely located on a business street in the colored section of the city that can be rented till next May for $17.50 per month. This hall can be made to seat about two hundred persons by moving the partition back a few feet. For comfort during the cold weather this partition should be extended to the ceiling. The Sabbath-keepers there have sent in to the committee tithes amounting to $20.00, and now they plan to provide for the heating and lighting of the hall from their tithes. The committee desires to secure the hall for the six months beginning November 1, for which we need at least $150.00 for rent and material for extending the partition. Then, too, we must either rent or purchase a piano for the meetings. Both Mr. and Mrs. Crichlow play the piano. And the committee should have sufficient funds during the year for postage for the correspondence of the department, and for such printing as is needful to carry on the work. And it would be very helpful to the cause if we could send Mr. Crichlow to visit groups of Sabbath-keeping colored people with whom we are corresponding in near-by cities.

The more the committee becomes acquainted with the possibilities of this work the more interested we get in it. We are seeking to move carefully and wisely,— *but we feel that we must move forward.* Brother and Sister Crichlow are going to reach many for good in their correspondence, and we must provide a place in which they can hold evangelistic and Sabbath meetings.

Doubtless there are other persons who, knowing more about the work will be glad to give a dollar a week, while in other cases groups of persons can join in paying the share, while Sabbath schools and Christian Endeavor societies can help financially in carrying on the work.

Members of the committee will be glad at any time to give information or answer questions about the work.

Funds for the work should be sent to Rev. James L. Skaggs, 511 Central Avenue, Plainfield, N. J.

WILLARD D. BURDICK,
Chairman.

425 *Center Street,*
Dunellen, N. J.

THE TEST OF A MAN

The test of a man is the fight he makes,
The grit that he daily shows;
The way he stands on his feet and takes
Fate's numerous bumps and blows.
A coward can smile when there's naught to fear,
When nothing his progress bars;
But it takes a man to stand up and cheer
When some other fellow stars.

It isn't the victory, after all,
But the fight that a brother makes;
The man who, driven against the wall,
Still stands up erect and takes
The blows of fate with his head held high,
Bleeding, and bruised, and pale,
Is the man who'll win in the by and by,
For he isn't afraid to fail.

It's the bumps you get, and the jolts you get,
And the shocks that your courage stands;
The hours of sorrow and vain regret,
The prize that escapes your hands,
That test your mettle and prove your worth;
It isn't the blows you deal,
But the blows you take on the good old earth,
That show if your stuff is real.
—*Selected.*

"To add yesterday's load to what you already carry makes a heavy burden. Put tomorrow's load on top of that and you can not support it."

1920 CENSUS, JERSEY CITY, NJ

DEPARTMENT OF COMMERCE—BUREAU OF THE CENSUS [D1—578]

FOURTEENTH CENSUS OF THE UNITED STATES: 1920—POPULATION

NAME OF INCORPORATED PLACE _Jersey City_

[class, as township, town, precinct, district, hundred, beat, etc. See instructions.] [Insert proper name and, also, the class of class, as city, village, town, or borough. See instructions.]

ENUMERATED BY ME ON THE _6th_ DAY OF _January_

PLACE OF ABODE				NAME	RELATION	TENURE		PERSONAL DESCRIPTION				CITIZENSHIP			EDUCATION			Place of birth of each person and parents of each person	
	House number	Number of dwelling	Number of family	of each person whose place of abode on January 1, 1920, was in this family.	Relationship of this person to the head of the family.	Home owned or rented	If owned, free or mortgaged	Sex	Color or race	Age at last birthday	Single, married, widowed, or divorced	Year of immigration to the United States	Naturalized or alien	If naturalized, year of naturalization	Attended school any time since Sept. 1, 1919	Whether able to read	Whether able to write	PERSON — Place of birth	Mother tongue
1	2	3	4	5	6	7	8	9	10	11	12	13	14	15	16	17	18	19	20
	23	17	69	Jendrowski Adam	Son			M	W	15	S				Yes	Yes	Yes	New Jersey	
				Mary	Daughter			F	W	13	S				Yes	Yes	Yes	New Jersey	
				Eva	Daughter			F	W	12	S				Yes	Yes	Yes	New Jersey	
				Stephen	Son			M	W	9	S				Yes	Yes	Yes	New Jersey	
				Edward	Son			M	W	7	S				Yes	Yes		New Jersey	
				John	Son			M	W	2	S							New Jersey	
			70	Nicholas George	Head	R		M	B	35	M	1923	Na 1919		Yes	Yes		British W.I. 1923	English
				Lillian	Wife			F	B	30	M	1905	Na 1919		Yes	Yes		New Jersey	
				Esther	Daughter			F	B	9	S				Yes	Yes	Yes	Newfoundland	
				Morton	Son			M	B	7	S				Yes	Yes	Yes	Mississippi	
				Alvin	Son			M	B	4	S							Tennessee	
		71		Warnick, William	Head	R		M	B	23	M				Yes	Yes		Ohio	
				Willie	Wife			F	B	23	M				Yes	Yes		Virginia	
				George	Son			M	B	5	S				Yes	Yes		Virginia	
				Naomi	Daughter			F	B	2	S							New Jersey	
				Jeanette	Daughter			F	B	3/12	S							New Jersey	
				Moss, Mannie	Mother-in-law			F	B	43	W					Yes	Yes		Virginia	
				Margaret	Sister-in-law			F	B	17	S					Yes	Yes		Virginia	
				Harman	Brother-in-law			M	B	10	S				Yes	Yes	Yes	Virginia	
				Viola	Sister-in-law			F	B	7	S				Yes	Yes	Yes	Virginia	
		72		Warnick, Franklin	Head	R		M	B	54	M					Yes	Yes		Pennsylvania	
				Alice	Wife			F	B	47	M					Yes	Yes		Virginia	
		73		Warnick, Pauline	Head	R		M	B	24	M				Yes	Yes		Ohio	
				Eva	Wife			F	B	20	M				Yes	Yes		Virginia	
				Jack	Son			M	B	2	S							New Jersey	
				Edward	Son			M	B	3/12	S							New Jersey	
				Mary	Boarder?			F	B	28	W				Yes	Yes		Pennsylvania	
	183	18	74	Judwinski Victor	Head	R		M	W	33	M	1910	Al		Yes	Yes		Poland	Polish
				Alice	Wife			F	W	22	M	1910	Al		Yes	Yes		Poland	Polish
				Wladek	Son			M	W	5	S							New Jersey	

1920 census shows Lillian, Cyril, and children living in Jersey City, New Jersey. near Lillian's father, Franklin, and many other Warnicks. It's interesting that there are several Polish people living in the same area, apparently an apartment building. Based on some research of the area, it appears the buildings at this census address—10th Street—are different today than those in 1920.

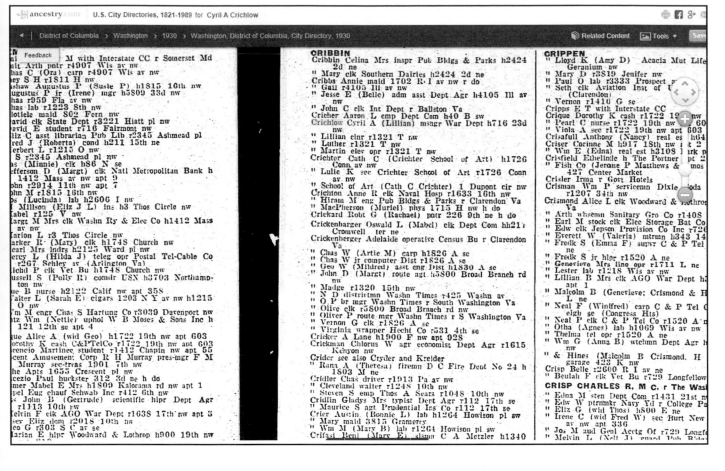

Above: 1930 city directory shows Cyril and Lillian and Luther and Martin living at two different locations during that year.

Right: The 1933 directory shows Cyril and Lillian living at two additional addresses! 1933 was the year that Lillian and Cyril officially divorced.

Below: Nashville City Directory 1914 showing Cyril as a student at Meharry Medical School. [Linda: Cyril did not finish Meharry. Nana (Lillian) used to tell of how Cyril wanted her to work while he attended school but she would not hear of that!]

1930 census page showing Cyril and Martin living at 654 Girard Street, NW. Census page shows Cyril's birthplace and his parents' birthplaces, and also shows Cyril's original immigration date of 1905.

CYRIL CRICHLOW DRAFT REGISTRATION CARD 1917

Chicago, Illinois June 5, 1917

1. Name: Cyril Askelon Crichlow
2. Address: 5205 Dearborn Chicago Illinois
3. Birth: September 12, 1889
4. Citizenship: Alien, Trinidad B.W.I.
5. Where Born: Trinidad, BWI
6. Nationality: British
7. Occupation: Editor
8. Employer: Half Century Magazine, 5202 S. Wabash Ave.
9. Dependents: Yes, Wife & Children
10. (Status) Married (Race) Negro
11. Prior military: None
12. Do you claim exemption from draft?: Alien, Wife, Religion

This is documentation that Cyril lived in Chicago, at least briefly. We don't know if Lillian and the children were with him or not.

This document, available in Ancestry.com, was brought to Linda's attention in an interesting way.

In June 2011, while attending the annual Juneteenth celebration sponsored by the Prince Georges County (MD) chapter of the African American Historical and Genealogy Society, I sat in on a workshop titled: Caribbean Immigrants, using Federal Records to Locate Ancestors from the British West Indians.

As the presenter, Damani Davis, archivist at the National Archives presented, he came to slides featuring Cyril Crichlow. All in the audience, including Damani, were surprised when I announced, "that's my grandfather!" Also included in Damani's presentation was a Passenger Arrivals List showing Cyril arriving in New York City from Trinidad. He probably had traveled to Trinidad for his father's funeral. Passenger Arrivals lists are among the documents available at the National Archives and Records Administration (NARA).

NOTES

p. 6. Tripp, S. "Lynchburg During the Civil War." *Encyclopedia Virginia*. Virginia Foundation for the Humanities, 31 May. 2011. Web. 28 Jul. 2014.

p. 18 Wormser, Richard. *"Rise and Fall of Jim Crow: Red Summer of 1919."* PBS. Public Broadcasting Company, 2002. Web. 12 Apr. 2014. <http://www.pbs.org/wnet/jimcrow/stories_events_red.html>.

There was indeed a race riot in 1919, immediately following WWI. With built up tensions following the war, "race riots" broke out in many cities and that year came to be known as the Red Summer. According to the Public Broadcasting station, the Red Summer refers to the summer and fall of 1919, in which race riots exploded in a number of cities in both the North and South. The three most violent episodes occurred in Chicago, Washington, DC, and Elaine, Arkansas. The 1919 riots in DC even touched on Ledroit Park where a man was pulled off a streetcar.

p. 25 Millners—A Store Full of Service. N.d. Photograph. Lynchburg, VA. *Lynch's Ferry*. Fall/Winter 2013 ed. Lynchburg, VA: Blackwell, 2013. Back Cover. Print.

p. 30 Jordan, Vernon E., and Annette Gordon-Reed. *Vernon Can Read!: A Memoir*. New York: Public Affairs, 2001. Print.

According to Vernon Jordan in *Vernon Can Read!,* when you "lived on the lot," you worked as a servant for a family and lived above the garage, in the basement or in some other space on their property.

p. 42 "Inspiration." *The* [Lynchburg] *News and Daily Advance*. Saturday, February 21, 1981.

p. 51. "Lees' Work Ethic Pays Off in Numerous Memories." *Page News and Courier*, Luray, VA, Thursday, May 5, 1994.

p. 53. Elizabeth and Clyde Lee both passed away in Luray, VA. Elizabeth in 1998. Clyde in 2006. Clyde Jr., Kenneth, Shellie, Mrs. Adams, Mr. Thompson and Aunt Eura have also passed.

p. 65 "Members of the Coordinating Committee for the Enforcement of the District of Columbia Anti-Discrimination Laws." courtesy Moorland-Spingarn Research Center, Howard University.

p. 67 "World Typing Champion Cortez W. Peters Opens First African-American Business College in Washington." The Washington Secretaries History Project. Online: http://washingtonsecretaries.blogspot.com. Accessed 7 April 2014.

p.79 Taylor, Woody. "Inside Your Government." *The Washington Afro-American* [Washington, DC] 30 Apr. 1949: Print.

p. 85 Photo of Lincoln Theater. Smith, Kathryn. Remembering U Street. online: http://www.meridianhilldc.org/ Accessed 4 April 2014.

p. 92 Crichlow-Braithwaite Shorthand School. Advertisement. *Negro World*. 21 Feb. 1921: n. page. Print.

page 93 GGJ: Good Government Job—Our neighbor and Georgetown Professor Dr. Maurice Jackson uses this term which I love. Many people, including African Americans, came to Washington after the Civil War where they could get jobs in the Federal Government. Even if the jobs were as elevator operators, maids or cleaners, these positions provided a (fairly) secure income, allowing them to purchase homes and educate their children and generally improve their quality of life.

p. 103 Thorngate, Janet. "Personality Profile: Lillian Crichlow." *The Sabbath Recorder* 200.3 March 1978, p. 8-9, 27. Print.

p. 107 Crichlow, Martha. "Rev. Luther Crichlow." *The Sabbath Recorder*. July 21, 1958, p. 13.

p. 109 "Archer-Crichlow Wedding is Brilliant Affair." *Baltimore Afro-American*, November 12, 1938. p. 8.

Print and Community Resources Cited

Alexandria City Public Library, Barrett Branch Local History Room, 717 Queen Street, Alexandria, VA 22314.

Amherst Virginia Historical Society. 154 South Main Street, Amherst, Virginia 24521.

Ancestry.com. U.S. City Directories, 1821-1989 [database on-line]. Provo, UT, USA: Ancestry.com Operations, Inc., 2011.

City Directories, Lynchburg, VA, 1881, 1885, 1900

City Directories, Washington, DC, 1930, 1933

City Directory, Nashville, TN, 1914

"Archer-Crichlow Wedding is Brilliant Affair." *Baltimore Afro-American*, November 12, 1938.

Conner, Paul and Ahmad Johnson. *African American Family Histories and Related Works in the Library of Congress*. Washington, DC: Library of Congress, 2009. PDF.

Corey, Charles., *History of the Richmond Theological Seminary*. Richmond, VA: J.W. Randolph, 1895. In *Black Biographical Dictionaries 1790-1950*. Alexandria, VA: Chadwyck-Healey, 1987. 162-63. Microfiche.

Craft, Shirley Thompson. *Four Families of Amherst and Nelson Counties, Virginia: Bolling/Bowling, Campbell, Massie, and Maddox: 1700s to Present*. Staunton, VA: Minuteman, 2002. Print.

Crichlow Braithwaite Shorthand School. Advertisement. Negro World 21 Feb. 1921: n. pag. Print.

Crichlow, Martha. "Rev. Luther Crichlow." *The Sabbath Recorder*. July 21, 1958, p. 13.

Davis, Damani. *"Caribbean Immigrants: Using Federal Records to Locate Ancestors from the West Indies: 1890-1930."* Juneteenth Celebration of the Afro-American

Historical and Genealogical Society. MD, Upper Marlboro. 18 June 2011. Lecture.

D.C. Public Library, Washingtoniana Division—City Directories, Tax records.

Elson, James M. *Lynchburg, Virginia: The First Two Hundred Years, 1786-1986*. Lynchburg, VA: Warwick House, 2004. Print.

Hughey, Robert. "East Boro Glimpses: Happenings in the Shadows of the Steel Mills." *The Pittsburgh Courier*, 9 Dec. 1939: 15. Print.

Elson, James M. "Lynchburg on the Eve of the War between the States." *Lynch's Ferry* Dec.-Jan. 1996: 12-23. Print.

"Inspiration." *The* [Lynchburg] *News and Daily Advance*. Saturday, February 21, 1981.

"Job Offered Teacher on Merged List." *The Washington Post and Times Herald* (1954-1959); Jul 15, 1954; ProQuest Historical Newspapers: The Washington Post (1877-1996) pg. 21.

Jones Memorial Library, 2311 Memorial Ave, Lynchburg, VA 24501.

Library of Congress Local History and Genealogy Reading Room, Washington, DC.

"Mary Kinney Obituary." *The Evening Star* [Washington, DC] 4 Jan. 1927: 9. The Evening Star. Web. 29 Apr. 2014.

McLeRoy, Sherrie, and William McLeRoy. *Passages: A History of Amherst County*. Lynchburg, VA: S.S. McLeRoy, 1977. Print.

"Members of the Coordinating Committee for the Enforcement of the District of Columbia Anti-Discrimination Laws." courtesy Moorland-Spingarn Research Center, Howard University.

Morales, Leslie Anderson, Ada Valaitis, Jennifer Learned, and Beverly Pierce. *Virginia Slave Births Index, 1853-1865*. Westminster, MD: Heritage, 2007. Print.

Nelson County Courthouse, 84 Courthouse Square, Lovingston, VA 22949-0010.

Nelson Memorial Library and Historical Society, 8521 Thomas Nelson Highway, Lovingston, VA 22949-0321.

Northrop, Henry Davenport, Joseph R. Gay, and I. Garland Penn. *The College of Life or Practical Self-educator: A Manual of Self-improvement for the Colored Race ... Giving Examples and Achievements of Successful Men and Women of the Race ... including Afro-American Progress Illustrated ...* Washington, DC: R. A. Dinsmore, 1896. Print.

Seventh Day Baptist Historical Society. Post Office Box 1678, Janesville, WI 53547-1678 http://www.sdbhistory.org/

Smith, Dorothy N. "Lee's Work Ethic Pays Off in Numerous Memories." *Page News and Courier* [Luray, VA] 5 May 1994: 9. Print.

Smith, Kathryn. The Lincoln Theater. ca 1950. Washington, DC. *"Remembering U Street."* Web. 14 Sept. 2013. http://www.meridianhilldc.org/.

"Talk O' Town, Crisp Breezy Comment on This and That and Those in Smoketown." *The Pittsburgh Courier*, 6 July 1935: 9. Pittsburgh Courier Online Archives. Web. 10 Nov. 2013.

Thorngate, Janet. "Personality Profile: Lillian Crichlow." *The Sabbath Recorder* (March 1978): 8-27. Print.

Virginia Bureau of Vital Statistics. [Registers of Births, deaths and marriages] 1853-1876. reel number 32. RELIC microfilm 929.3755 VIR.

"World Typing Champion Cortez W. Peters Opens First African-American Business College in Washington." The Washington Secretaries History Project. Online: http://washingtonsecretaries.blogspot.com. Accessed 7 April 2014.

For Further Reading, Annotated

One of the primary purposes of *Back There, Then* is to illustrate the achievements of African Americans despite the odds and to dispel common myths. All of the books on this list accomplish this, and each book tells stories of real people. Too often, history books speak only in generalities.

Baker, John F. *The Washingtons of Wessyngton Plantation: Stories of My Family's Journey to Freedom*. New York: Atria, 2009. Print.

A descendant of Wessyngton slaves, Baker has written the most accessible and exciting work of African American history since *Roots*. He has not only written his own family's story but included the history of hundreds of slaves and their descendants now numbering in the thousands throughout the United States. More than one hundred rare photographs and portraits of African Americans who were slaves on the plantation bring this compelling American history to life. Linda had the opportunity to visit Wessyngton and meet John Baker at the 2013 African American Historical and Genealogical Society meeting in Nashville, TN. Baker and his story bring an important perspective to our history.

Brumfield, Elizabeth Jean. *An Ordinary Man: Black Power in Overalls*. Houston, TX: Blurb, 2012. Print.

Brumfield, a university librarian, wrote this book about her father, a plumber in Pittsburgh, who, during segregation, was denied admittance to the plumber's union but later achieved prominence in his field. The Brumfield story mirrors somewhat that of Martin Crichlow. Crichlow initially did not receive the promotions he merited, but after advocating for himself and others, became the first Black foreman plumber in the General Services Administration.

Cauble, Frank P. *Biography of Wilmer Mc Lean*. Lynchburg, VA: H.E. Howard, 1987. Print.

Wilmer McLean is the man we understand to be the father of Lucy Glover, Marietta's great-grandmother. It was in his home that Lee surrendered to Grant at Appomattox, essentially ending the Civil War.

Clarkson-Turpeau, Brenda. *Almost Forgotten: The Real America*. Atlanta, GA: 3T Unlimited, 2011. Print.

One of the wonderful family stories which illustrates black achievements and helps dispel racial myths.

Du Bois, W. E. B. *The Souls of Black Folk*. New York: New American Library, 1969. Print.

Du Bois' book is one of the classics of black literature by the person whose tactical approach to racial uplift was philosophically "different" from that of Booker T. Washington. It is an autobiographical and historical collection of essays which explore a variety of racial themes. Perhaps the most famous theme involves the notion of 'double consciousness,' the idea that African Americans' perceptions of themselves are often based on the ways in which white Americans look at them.

Franklin, John Hope. *Mirror to America: The Autobiography of John Hope Franklin*. New York: Farrar, Straus and Giroux, 2005. Print.

Like Marietta Crichlow, John Hope Franklin lived through America's most defining twentieth-century transformation, the dismantling of legally protected racial segregation. Franklin was the "dean" of African American scholars. On the cover of this book, he is simply described as an "American scholar." This, like Franklin's *From Slavery to Freedom*, is a must-read for a full understanding of African American life in the 20th century.

Gordon-Reed, Annette. *The Hemingses of Monticello: An American Family*. New York, NY: W.W. Norton, 2009. Print.

She is the historian who brought widespread legitimacy to the existence of a liaison between Thomas Jefferson and his slave Sally Hemings. This award-winning book continues that story through an exploration of multiple generations of Hemings' family.

Haizlip, Shirlee Taylor. *The Sweeter the Juice: A Family Memoir in Black and White*. New York: Touchstone, 1995. Print.

Shirlee Taylor Haizlip, in an effort to reconcile the dissonance between her black persona and her undeniably multiracial heritage, started on a journey of discovery that took her over thousands of miles and hundreds of years. While searching for her mother's family, Haizlip confronted the deeply intertwined but often ignored tensions regarding skin color among blacks.

Haley, Alex. *Roots*. Garden City, NY: Doubleday, 1976. Print.

One of the most important books and television series ever to appear, *Roots* is the saga of an African American family, which begins in Africa. It galvanized the nation, and created an extraordinary political, racial, social and cultural dialogue. The book sold over one million copies in the first year, and the miniseries was watched by an astonishing 130 million people. It also won both the Pulitzer Prize and the National Book Award. *Roots* inspired people of all races to research and reflect on their own family histories.

Hill, Robert A., and Marcus Garvey. *The Marcus Garvey and Universal Negro Improvement Association Papers*. Vol. 8. Durham, NC: Duke UP, 2011. Print.

In this book about Marcus Garvey, Hill includes details about Cyril Crichlow's involvement with Garvey.

James, Beatrice Pierce. *Let Every Day Be Your Best Day*. Northlight, 2012. Print.

Appomattox, Virginia, native James shares information about her family history through exceptional-quality photos and stories.

Lanier, Shannon, and Jane Feldman. *Jefferson's Children: The Story of One American Family*. New York: Random House, 2000. Print.

This is included in the list not only because Shannon was one of Kwame White's roommates in college but because it is an easy-to-read book that describes the Black and White descendants of Thomas Jefferson. The book shows, via real people in Shannon's family, how blacks can be descended from whites and how folks who think they are white might be descended from blacks. Shannon is one of the black descendants of Jefferson.

LaRoche, Cheryl Janifer. *Free Black Communities and the Underground Railroad: The Geography of Resistance*. Urbana, IL: University of Illinois, 2014. Print.

Cheryl's book chronicles the life of free black communities in the 19th century, many of whom were like our families then and now. For those seeking a deeper understanding of African American history, it includes a very extensive bibliography.

Lucas, Patricia. *Whitehead Family*. Utica, KY: McDowell Publications, 2003.

Historical sketch and genealogy of the Mark Whitehead family (originally from Georgia), that eventually dropped the ending of their name, "head" and became White, the ancestors of Eric White, husband of Linda Crichlow White. The early generations of this family had 10 or more children, so there are lots of cousins and the family comes together biennially for family reunions in various parts of the USA. Much credit is due to Pat for documenting the family tree and for inspiring Linda and others to research their family history.

The Smithsonian Anacostia Museum and Center for African American History and Culture. *The Black Washingtonians: The Anacostia Museum Illustrated Chronology*. Hoboken NJ: Wiley, 2005. Print.

Including extensive illustrations, this book presents the reader with a timeline of the contributions of African American—both known and unknown—from the time of the city's birth through the present. Eleanor Holmes Norton, D.C. Delegate to the U.S. House of Representatives, observes in a forward that both the achievements and setbacks of the nation's capitol are legacies which must be recognized.

Stewart, Alison. *First Class: The Legacy of Dunbar, America's First Black Public High School*. Chicago: Chicago Review, 2013. Print.

Many believe Stewart's book to be the definitive account of Dunbar High School and its predecessors, renowned for the exemplary education provided by and for African Americans in segregated Washington, DC, from 1870 through the 1950s.

Washburn, Patrick Scott. *The African American Newspaper: Voice of Freedom*. Evanston, IL: Northwestern UP, 2006. Print.

Linda had an interesting experience as a school librarian. While attending a workshop on library databases in about 2005, one of the vendors described his database as consisting of 19th century newspapers that had been scanned in cooperation with the American Antiquarian Society. When I asked him if Black newspapers were included, his response was "Were there any?"

So, here was a professional who did not know that Black newspapers existed in the 19th century. Similarly, when I talked to my students about early black newspapers such as Freedom's Journal, published in New York 1827 by Samuel Cornish and John Russworm, their response is "we thought Black people weren't allowed to read and write back then."

Indeed, this is a common fallacy. However, it's important that readers of this book understand that Black newspapers have long been a part of our community. These papers might have been church newspapers, organization newsletters such as those of the Prince Hall Masons, school alumni associations, or the more widely read ones, The Chicago Daily Defender, The Pittsburg Courier or The Afro-American.

Whatever the format, they performed an important community service. And, it's important to note that throughout slavery, many African Americans could read and write. Some were never slaves. John Russworm learned to read and write in his native Jamaica. Some, such as Frederick Douglass, claim to have been self-taught.

Many of the Stevens, Garland, and Crichlow events were noted in the black press. As you continue the genealogy quest, remember to search through Black newspapers.

Washington, Booker T. *Up from Slavery: Booker T. Washington*. New York, NY: Airmont Pub., 1967. Print.

The classic story of pulling oneself up by one's bootstraps. Marietta gave it to Linda to read when Linda was in junior high school. Many of the people in our family as well as the people in some of the other family stories in this bibliography were educated at Hampton Institute (later University) or Tuskegee Institute in the Booker T. Washington tradition. This book has been in print since it was first serialized in 1900, and has been listed as one of the most important non-fiction books of the 20th century.

Wilkerson, Isabel. *The Warmth of Other Suns: The Epic Story of America's Great Migration*. New York, NY: Random House, 2010. Print.

Pulitzer Prize–winning author Isabel Wilkerson chronicles one of the great stories of American history: the decades-long migration of black citizens who fled the South for northern and western cities, in search of a better life—other suns. Wilkerson grew up in the Petworth neighborhood of Washington and attended Roosevelt High School a few years after Linda. While many books have been written about the Black migration, this one is the best, giving names and personal experiences to the stories.

Williams, Edward Christopher, Adam McKible, and Emily Bernard. *When Washington Was in Vogue: A Love Story (a Lost Novel of the Harlem Renaissance)*. New York, NY: Amistad, 2003. Print.

Although this is fiction, it provides a wonderful description of what life was like for upwardly mobile African Americans in Washington the 1920s. It is one of the few, if not the only, book written about Negroes at that time that doesn't pit them against White folks. In fact, there are no Whites in the novel. A delightful story! An interesting element here is that, despite chronicling the character's daily lives, there is never any mention of the folks in this story going to church. The Stevens and the Crichlows and probably most other colored people in Washington would have attended church during the 1920s.

Williams, Minnie Simons. *A Colloquial History of A Black South Carolina Family Named Simons*. Self Published. 1990.

A family story that features the Glen Simons branch. Lillian Crichlow's sister Naomi married Glen Simons. Josephine Simons Wade, one of our DC family friends and member of the Mother-Daughter club with Marietta and . Linda is also part of this family and is featured therein.

Willis, Deborah. *Posing Beauty: African American Images, from the 1890s to the Present*. New York, NY: W.W. Norton, 2009. Print.

Posing Beauty features, on page 108, one of the Charles Bruce photos that was found in cousin Constance Bruce's home in 2006. Willis is one of the nation's leading historians of African American photography and curators of African American culture. Her books and other resources can be helpful to the genealogist.

Index

162